Yellowstone and Grand Teton National Parks Road Guide

THE ESSENTIAL GUIDE FOR MOTORISTS

by
Jeremy Schmidt (Grand Teton)

and
Steven Fuller (Yellowstone)

NATIONAL GEOGRAPHIC
WASHINGTON, D.C.

The National Geographic Society is one of the world's
largest nonprofit scientific and educational organizations.
Founded in 1888 to "increase and diffuse geographic knowl-
edge," the Society works to inspire people to care about the
planet. It reaches more than 325 million people worldwide
each month through its official journal, *National Geographic,*
and other magazines; National Geographic Channel;
television documentaries; music; radio; films; books; DVDs;
maps; exhibitions; school publishing programs; interactive
media; and merchandise. National Geographic has funded
more than 9,000 scientific research, conservation
and exploration projects and supports an education pro-
gram combating geographic illiteracy.

For more information, please call 1-800-NGS LINE
(647-5463) or write to the following address:

National Geographic Society
1145 17th Street N.W.
Washington, D.C. 20036-4688 U.S.A.

Visit us online at www.nationalgeographic.com

Contents

How to Use This Guide   5

The Greater Yellowstone Ecosystem   6

Travelers' Information   8

Yellowstone: America's Original Park   14

    Great Fires of 1988   16
    Road Maps   18–68

**Grand Teton: Shining Lakes
    and Granite Towers**   70

    Road Maps   74-92

Index   94

Further Reading   95

"Monday, September 19, 1870…We had within a distance of fifty miles seen what we believed to be the greatest wonders on the continent. Judge then, of our astonishment on entering this basin, to see at no great distance before us an immense body of sparkling water, projected suddenly and with terrific force into the air to a height of over one hundred feet. We had found a real geyser. In the valley before us were a thousand hot springs of various sizes and character, and five hundred craters jetting forth vapor…

"We gave such names to those of the geysers which we saw in action as we think will best illustrate their peculiarities. The one I have just described General Washburn has named 'Old Faithful,' because of the regularity of its eruption."

—N. P. Langford, member of the 1870
Washburn–Langford–Doane Expedition
and Yellowstone's first superintendent

"There are many peaks in the Rockies as lofty as the Teton, but beyond this point all parallelism ceases.

"The country surrounding the peaks is rugged and wild beyond the power of words to convey, and when the region becomes more accessible, by means of railroads already projected, it will doubtless rival, as a pleasuring ground, the famous [Yellowstone] National Park itself."

—William Owen, after an unsuccessful
1891 attempt to climb the Grand Teton.
He did climb it in 1898, with the Spalding Party,
officially the first ascent.

How to Use This Guide

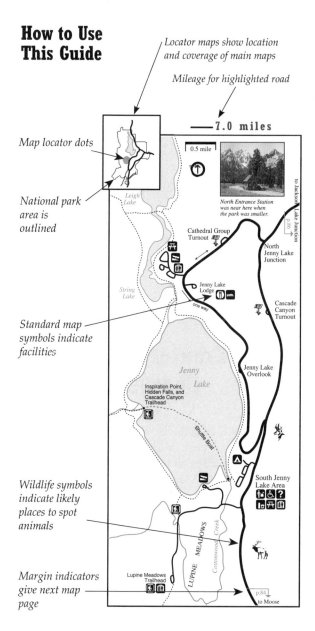

Locator maps show location and coverage of main maps

Mileage for highlighted road

— 7.0 miles

Map locator dots

National park area is outlined

0.5 mile

North Entrance Station was near here when the park was smaller.

Leigh Lake

to Jackson Lake Junction

p. 86

Cathedral Group Turnout

North Jenny Lake Junction

Jenny Lake Lodge

Cascade Canyon Turnout

String Lake

one way

Standard map symbols indicate facilities

Jenny Lake Overlook

Jenny Lake

Inspiration Point, Hidden Falls, and Cascade Canyon Trailhead

Shuttle Boat

South Jenny Lake Area

Wildlife symbols indicate likely places to spot animals

LUPINE MEADOWS

Cottonwood Creek

Margin indicators give next map page

Lupine Meadows Trailhead

p. 84

to Moose

- Key maps inside front (Yellowstone) and back (Grand Teton) covers give page numbers for road maps.

- Map features and commentary run side by side.

- Maps are generally in sequence. Page numbers for adjoining maps are given in map margins. Or refer to locator maps or key maps.

- This book is a guide for motorists, not hikers or other backcountry users, who will find topographic maps and trail guides essential.

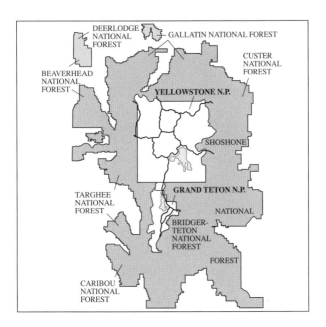

The Greater Yellowstone Ecosystem

YOU CAN SEE IT in satellite photos—a high, mostly forested land, punctuated by sharp mountains and bounded by semiarid plains. Biologists call it the Greater Yellowstone Ecosystem, a region defined by climate and geography, not by administrative decree. Yellowstone and Grand Teton National Parks form only the heart of it. The ecosystem sprawls across three states, seven national forests, almost a dozen federally designated wilderness areas, various other reserves, and a substantial amount of private land. The states, the federal government, county governments, and local communities all have responsibilities for the area.

The concept of Greater Yellowstone recognizes that the individual parks and forests are not distinct units, but rather part of a large interconnected whole. Grizzly bears, swans, bison, and other animals move through it according to ancient imperatives, not recognizing the borders. Not so long ago, all this was theirs, a splendid, seamless wild land.

Now, chopped into a variety of jurisdictions, sliced by a network of highways, back roads, and other developments, its best winter range occupied by cattle ranches and towns, the ecosystem is threatened and its integrity compromised.

Yellowstone is large, but not large enough for the bison who migrate out of the park to their ancient wintering grounds and into conflict with a variety of state, local, and federal interests. The Teton Wilderness seems enormous until thousands of elk

Opposite: The Greater Yellowstone Ecosystem comprises two national parks, seven national forests, many designated wilderness areas, several wildlife refuges, and parts of three states.

come streaming out of the high country into Jackson Hole each November. The elk find their migration routes cut off by towns, highways, and ranches, and spend the winter bunched together on one large refuge. The same geographic concerns hold true for all creatures that move with the seasons, including eagles, swans, cranes, bighorn sheep; or those that range over large areas, like coyotes, wolves, grizzlies, pronghorn, and others. They all need more space than any one administrative unit can provide.

Even plants move, although more slowly than animals. Exotic "weeds" are an obvious example, being brought in by domestic animals or by human activity. Over a period of millennia, as ice ages and droughts have come and gone, so have trees and shrubs and flowers, reflecting the concept that they are only component parts of the great, interwoven fabric of life.

From an administrative point of view, the concept of this ecosystem underscores the need for cooperation. People from Caribou National Forest need to talk with their counterparts on Gallatin, and in Yellowstone, and on private ranches, and so forth. Awareness is growing, but there is a long way to go before human management catches up with natural processes.

For the visitor, Greater Yellowstone is more than an interesting concept. It also means that activities should not be limited to the national parks. Camping, fishing, wildlife viewing, boating, and just about any other outdoor activity can be pursued throughout the region. Few roads in the world rival the Beartooth Highway, which crosses 10,940-foot Beartooth Pass near Yellowstone's northeast corner. Backpackers find the Wind River Range trails to be some of the best. Back roads lead to remote campsites throughout the region, some with picnic tables and pit toilets, others entirely primitive. The best way to explore these back roads is with detailed maps printed by the various national forests, available at Forest Service ranger stations and national park visitor centers, along with other information.

Travelers' Information

VISITOR CENTERS provide books, maps, permits, and general information. In Yellowstone, visitor centers are located at Mammoth, Norris, Canyon, Old Faithful, Fishing Bridge, and Grant Village; in Grand Teton, at Moose and Colter Bay.

Entrance permits good for seven days in both parks cost $25 per private vehicle and $12 per person for those entering by other means (bicycle, commercial bus, or foot). A $50 permit provides access for one year to both Yellowstone and Grand Teton. The Interagency Annual Pass costs $50 and covers national parks and other Interior Department sites. Golden Age Passports (for persons over 62) cost $10, a onetime fee. Golden Access Passports (for handicapped persons) are free. Both passports provide park admission and reduced camping fees.

Correspondence should be directed to park headquarters: Yellowstone National Park, P.O. Box 168, Yellowstone National Park, WY 82190 (tel. 307-344-7381) *www.nps.gov/yell;* or Grand Teton National Park, P.O. Drawer 170, Moose, WY 83012 (tel. 307-739-3300) *www.nps.gov/grte.*

Driving: Except where otherwise posted, the speed limit in both parks is 45 mph. Some side roads are not suitable for RVs. Gasoline is available in Yellowstone at most road junctions and entrances; in Teton, at

Colter Bay, Moose Village, Signal Mountain Lodge, and at Flagg Ranch on the north boundary. Services are limited in spring and fall. Diesel can be had in Teton at Colter Bay and Jackson Lake Lodge; in Yellowstone at Mammoth, Canyon, Grant, and Old Faithful.

Opposite: Rocky Mountain gray wolves, reintroduced to Yellowstone in 1996, mark the return of a key species to the ecosystem.

Boating: For private boats, seven-day permits ($5; $10 if motorized) and annual permits ($10; $20 if motorized) are honored by both parks, with certain conditions. For example, a Teton permit is good in Yellowstone, but boaters are still required to check in at a Yellowstone ranger station for a non-fee tag before going on the water. In Yellowstone, boats are permitted only on lakes, not rivers, except for the channel between Lewis and Shoshone Lakes. Motors are permitted only on Yellowstone and Lewis Lakes; parts of Yellowstone Lake are off-limits to motorboats.

In Grand Teton, the Snake River, running fast and cold along the base of the mountains, may be floated in non-motorized craft. Although not a white-water run, the currents are tricky and snags can be a serious hazard to boaters not familiar with western rivers. Jackson, Jenny, and Phelps Lakes are open to motorboats (8-mph limit on Jenny). Other lakes—Emma Matilda, Two Ocean, Taggart, Bradley, Bearpaw, Leigh, and String—are open only to canoes and other hand-propelled craft. Boat rentals are available on Jackson and Jenny Lakes in Teton; at Bridge Bay and Grant Village in Yellowstone.

Fishing: In Yellowstone, a permit is required ($20 for 7 days; $35 for the season; age 15 and under, free). In Grand Teton, fishermen must carry a Wyoming fishing license. Regulations in both parks are designed to protect fish populations. Rules are complicated and change from one area to the next. Catch-and-release fly-fishing with barbless hooks is encouraged and in some places required.

Hiking: Even at the height of the summer season, when park roads are most crowded, all it takes to find peace is to park the car and walk down a trail—into the forest, through a meadow, along a riverbank, into the solace of wildness.

No permit is required for day hiking in either park, but a few common-sense precautions are in order. Don't go alone. Carry a trail map. Be prepared for sudden weather changes. Summer thunderstorms are common. Snow can fall in any month.

Mountaineering: Climbing in the Teton Range can be rewarding but dangerous. Safety demands training, judgment, and proper equipment. Instruction and guide service are available from The Exum School of American Mountaineering, P.O. Box 56, Moose, WY 83012 (tel. 307- 733-2297); or Jackson Hole Mountain Guides, P.O. Box 7477, Jackson, WY 83002 (tel. 307-734-4979).

Horseback Riding: Guided horseback rides are available in both parks. In Yellowstone there are stables at Canyon Village, Roosevelt Lodge, and Mammoth Hot Springs; in Teton, at Jenny Lake, Colter Bay, and Jackson Lake Lodge. Guest ranches operate in the vicinity of both parks.

Handicapped Access: Both parks provide activities and access for disabled persons. All visitor centers, some rest rooms, some ranger-led activities, most roadside viewpoints, and many exhibits are wheelchair accessible or accessible with assistance.

Wildlife: The Yellowstone-Teton region remains the richest wildlife preserve in the United States outside of Alaska. Animals found here form a compendium of Rocky Mountain wildlife: elk, deer, moose, bighorn sheep, mountain goats, bison (commonly called buffalo), pronghorn (also called antelope), grizzly and black bears, mountain lions, coyotes, and, since their reintroduction in 1996, Rocky Mountain gray wolves. Prominent birds include trumpeter swans, white pelicans, bald and golden eagles, sandhill cranes, Canada geese, osprey, and many more.

Viewing of wildlife should be done with sensitivity for the animals. Most will not tolerate being approached too closely, and some will defend themselves if they feel threatened. Every year, park visitors are injured and sometimes killed by wild animals that only appear tame. Generally, if your presence causes any animal to change its behavior, you are too close.

Seasons: Many roads close for the winter. In Yellowstone, only the northern highway from Gardiner, Montana, to Cooke City, Montana, is kept plowed. The other park roads are open only for oversnow vehicles. In Grand Teton, the inner park road is closed from Cottonwood Creek north to Jackson Lake Dam. The main road, however, from Jackson, Wyoming, all the way to Flagg Ranch near the south boundary of Yellowstone, is kept open all winter—a spectacular drive on a sunny, snowbound morning.

Most roads in both parks are usually open for the season by the end of April, although snowbanks linger into June and beyond. Spring is a time of unsettled weather; days of rain and wet snow are common.

Summer, by local reckoning, begins on the Fourth of July, and ends, two days later. In fact, it lasts almost two months—a short time, cherished by all who visit the Rockies, but particularly by residents who try to get their fill of warmth before the return of winter.

Fall slides gradually out of summer. Grasses turn golden. Days stay warm but nights are cool. By the middle of September there is frost each night. Autumn is an exciting time in the mountains. Wildlife is more easily visible than in summer. Elk, moose, and deer have grown full antlers; for them, this is mating season. Elk especially are evident, their bugling calls ringing through frosty meadows.

Occasional snowstorms move across the parks in October, but they leave only traces of white on the high peaks. The big storms arrive in November, and then winter begins in earnest—deep, cold, and beautiful.

Lodging: Accommodations are available in both parks and in surrounding communities. During summer, lodging is often fully booked. For the Teton area contact: Grand Teton Lodge Co., P.O. Box 240, Moran, WY 83013 (tel. 307-543-2811 or 800-628-9988); Signal Mountain Lodge, P.O. Box 50, Moran, WY 83013 (tel. 307-543-2831); Flagg Ranch Village, P.O. Box 187, Moran, WY 83013 (tel. 307-543-2861 or 800-443-2311 outside of Wyoming); Dornan's Spur Ranch (at Moose, tel. 307-733-2522); or Jackson Hole Chamber of Commerce, P.O. Box E, Jackson, WY 83001 (tel. 307-733-3316). For Yellowstone lodging contact: Xanterra Parks and Resorts, Yellowstone National Park, WY 82190 (tel. 307-344-7311).

Campgrounds: Campgrounds in both Yellowstone and Grand Teton provide basic services: tent pads, picnic tables, toilets, drinking water, and trash collection. Most campsites cost $18 to $20 per night.

Special regulations are posted in the official park brochures. For example, as a precaution against bears, tenting is not permitted at Yellowstone's Canyon Campground. Jenny Lake Campground in Grand Teton, on the other hand, is reserved for tents only. Some campgrounds have special sites reserved for hikers and bicyclists. Reservations can be made through Xanterra (tel. 866-439-7375) for some campgrounds in Yellowstone; others are first come, first served. During busy summer months, all sites might be taken by noon. No roadside camping is permitted.

There are many excellent campgrounds in the national forests surrounding the parks. Maintained by the Forest Service, these are often less crowded and more secluded than sites inside the parks.

Hookups are available only in campgrounds outside the parks, with two exceptions: the privately operated RV parks at Fishing Bridge in Yellowstone and Colter Bay in Teton; reserve through Xanterra or Grand Teton Lodge Company (see p. 11).

It's against the law to feed wild animals. Getting food from people changes an animal's natural behavior, often in harmful ways. Especially in the case of bears and coyotes, the connection between people and food can become a dangerous one—for the animals and for the public. The objective of park regulations is to maintain conditions that are as natural as possible, where animals live their lives as they would if people were not present. Except when preparing or eating meals, food must be kept securely locked in your vehicle, preferably in the trunk. Put all trash in the bear-resistant trash cans found along park roads and in campgrounds.

Pets: Pets are permitted on leash, and only near paved roads; never in the backcountry, on nature trails, or in buildings.

Emergencies: In Yellowstone call 911, or call the rangers at park headquarters, 307-344-7381. In Grand Teton call 911 or the rangers at 307-739-3301.

On the Road

Yellowstone: America's Original Park

STRADDLING the Continental Divide in the mountains of northwest Wyoming, Yellowstone sits atop a rare geologic hot spot, where molten rock rises close to the surface. Occasionally it breaks through, as it did about 600,000 years ago in a catastrophic eruption that resulted in a great caldera, or collapsed volcano, some 28 by 47 miles across. Things are relatively quiet today, but the ground remains hot. Water from rain and melting snow percolates into the earth until it encounters the volcanic heat far below and is driven back toward the surface to form geysers and hot springs.

Most of the park is situated on a plateau with an average elevation of 8,000 feet, ringed on three sides by mountain ranges 2,000 to 3,000 feet higher. The Yellowstone Plateau is a gentle rounded landscape of forest and meadow animated by an abundance of wildlife living amid great lakes, canyons, and cold crystalline streams. Protected since it was declared a national park in 1872, Yellowstone recalls North America as it was before industrial man arrived and profoundly transformed the continent.

Yellowstone does not boast the spectacular alpine scenery of Glacier National Park or the breathtaking voids of the Grand Canyon. A quick trip along its roads may leave the casual visitor wondering, "Where's the scenery?" Yellowstone's beauty is subtle and its delights are deep, but they require time to appreciate.

Since the end of the Ice Age, 10,000 years ago, well-worn animal trails led Stone Age hunters into the heart of the Yellowstone country. In the 19th century, extended family groups of horse-mounted Indians came here to camp in summer, perhaps for much the same reason modern Americans visit here.

In the early 1800s, fur trappers were the first non-natives in the area—John Colter, Jim Bridger, Osborne Russell, and others. A few prospectors ventured through in later years, but no one took serious notice of the park until 1870 when General Washburn led a party of Montanans to the plateau. Their report resulted in the official Hayden Expedition of 1871; members included artist Thomas Moran and photographer W. H. Jackson, whose work helped convince Congress that this place was an extraordinary wonder in a continent filled with wonders.

Yellowstone was declared a national park in 1872, four years before the battle at Little Bighorn, a couple hundred miles to the east of the park. The continent was then a raw land and America was a brash young nation that could imagine no limits, which makes it especially remarkable that the park was ever created in the first place. No one even knew what a national park should be. The original act termed it a "public park or pleasureing-ground."

Yellowstone was set aside chiefly for its geysers and natural oddities. In 1872, wildlife was abundant throughout the West. Now, however, the park's creatures—elk, deer, moose, bears, bison (buffalo), pronghorn (antelope), eagles, pelicans, swans, bighorn sheep, trout, coyotes, mountain lions, wolves, and more—are cherished by visitors. New qualities, of which we are today unaware, may become treasures in the future.

Yellowstone represents one of the great inventions of American culture, an invention that has become an inspiration and a model for the rest of the world. In Yellowstone, for the first time in history, the citizens of a country set aside a large tract of land and began to consider self-imposed limitations on how to exploit its natural bounty. We may hope that this tradition will be expanded and that our ongoing national love affair with Yellowstone may help us in our quest to find a sustainable relationship with all of nature and the planet.

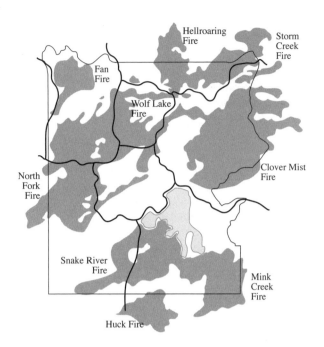

Map labels: Hellroaring Fire, Storm Creek Fire, Fan Fire, Wolf Lake Fire, Clover Mist Fire, North Fork Fire, Snake River Fire, Mink Creek Fire, Huck Fire

Great Fires of 1988

DURING the summer of 1988, eight wildfires swept Yellowstone, burning 793,880 acres, or 36 percent of the total area of the park. They made up the biggest group of fires in the northern Rockies in 50 years. About 25,000 firefighters worked the area, while dozens of helicopters, and more than 100 fire trucks were deployed to protect developed areas at a cost of about $120 million—the most expensive fire fight in history.

By autumn, snow and rain had doused the last of the fires, leaving great expanses of blackened landscape. Yet even before the first heavy snows of winter covered the park, green shoots of new growth were beginning to emerge from the ashes. Spring brought with it an impressive display of how natural systems cope with fire. In the years since then, one of the more interesting aspects of a visit to Yellowstone has been the opportunity to trace the story of its great fires.

The largest fire in Yellowstone was the North Fork Fire, which burned some 400,000 acres. It was started June 22 by a woodcutter just west of the park. Over the course of the summer it threatened developments at Old Faithful, Madison, Norris, Canyon, Mammoth, Tower-Roosevelt, and the towns of West Yellowstone and Gardiner, Montana, just outside the park's west and north boundaries.

On hot windy days during that unforgettable summer, big fires ran as far as 13 miles in a day. Winds gusting over 60 miles an hour threw embers one to two miles ahead of the fire front, triggering yet more fires. Fires jumped highways, rivers, and even the Grand Canyon of the Yellowstone River, not to mention fire lines cleared through the forest to the width of nine bulldozer blades.

Opposite: Shaded areas indicate, in broad outline, the extent of the 1988 fires. The intensity of burning varied considerably with location, and large areas within these perimeters were not burned at all. Other areas showed no evidence of fire effects just one year later—an interesting aspect of traveling through post-fire Yellowstone.

Many people were fearful of what the fires had done to the wildlife in the park. How many animals had died in the holocaust? A systematic survey, begun immediately after the fires, revealed a total of 264 large mammals had been killed: 246 elk, two moose, four mule deer, nine bison, two grizzly bears, and one black bear. About 30,000 elk summer here, while 2,500 bison, 2,500 mule deer, 200 moose, 250 grizzly bears, and 500 black bears are year-round residents.

Most of the wildlife victims died of smoke asphyxiation. In addition, firefighting vehicles collided with and killed 108 large mammals in road accidents. The total numbers, however sad, were insignificant in terms of animal population dynamics.

Some visitors saw only pitiful devastation in the aftermath of the burning. But nature has her own agenda and Yellowstone, first and foremost, is a nature preserve, a place in which natural processes can unfold without undue interference from man. Fires have a creative as well as a destructive side. Fire greatly hastens the metabolism of the Rocky Mountain forest. All those burned trees did not go to waste in the sense that their ashes nourished the soil that produced the trees to begin with. Yellowstone's landscape is one born from fire, shaped and modified by a series of forest fires going back as long as trees have grown here.

As a result of the fires, Yellowstone today is a sunnier, more open place, richer in animal habitat and plant diversity than it was before 1988. There is no real destruction in nature, only transformation and the slow recycling of riches. The notion of fire as a creative force is a difficult lesson to learn, one that seems to contradict common sense, but it is a profound lesson, and one of the greatest gifts Yellowstone has to offer us.

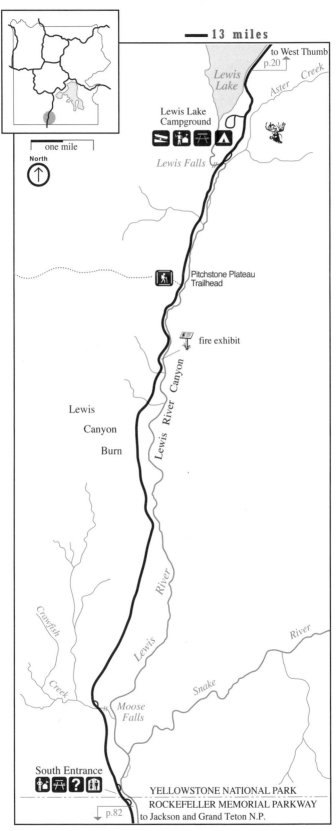

13 miles

to West Thumb
p.20

Lewis Lake

Aster Creek

Lewis Lake
Campground

Lewis Falls

Pitchstone Plateau
Trailhead

fire exhibit

Lewis River Canyon

Lewis

Canyon

Burn

River

Lewis

Crawfish

Snake

River

Creek

Moose Falls

South Entrance

YELLOWSTONE NATIONAL PARK
ROCKEFELLER MEMORIAL PARKWAY
to Jackson and Grand Teton N.P.

p.82

one mile

North

South Entrance to West Thumb

Lewis River Falls: The 30-foot-high falls are just upstream of the highway bridge, where Aster Creek flows into the Lewis River. The bottomland here is rich with willows, favorite browse of the many moose that live in the area.

Lewis River Canyon: Although the river was named for Meriwether Lewis of the Lewis and Clark Expedition of 1804-06, the Corps of Discovery never entered Yellowstone. Clark, on the return journey, passed about 50 miles north near present-day Livingston, Montana. The Lewis River joins the Snake on its flow to the Pacific just north of the south entrance to the park. This canyon, 600 feet deep and 1.5-miles long, lies where two black rhyolite lava flows joined about half a million years ago. The Tetons are visible to the south, the Absaroka Range to the east.

Fire Exhibit—Firepower: There are many varieties of forest fire, from crown fires (when wind-driven fire sweeps through the canopy), to cool, slow ground burns. Here the fire burned hot and fast. Driven by high winds and drought conditions, flames jumped the 500-yard-wide natural barrier of the Lewis River Canyon. In other areas, bulldozer lines seemed puny in the face of the awesome fire storms of the summer of 1988.

Lodgepole Tunnel: The road seems like a tunnel where it passes through a mature lodgepole forest. Lodgepoles, which grow straight and slender, were used as tepee poles. In Yellowstone they grow slowly—as a rule of thumb one inch of trunk thickness per decade. The road follows the south side of Pitchstone Plateau, a pile of lava more than 2,000 feet high and about 20 miles across, created in the aftermath of the eruption of the great Yellowstone caldera. The caldera crater measured 28 by 47 miles and was a half-mile deep. The eruption is largely responsible for the Yellowstone landscape as we know it today.

Moose Falls: The creek that pours over this 30-foot-high falls is warmed by hot springs—crawfish live in its waters, unusual at this latitude and altitude.

South Entrance: (Elev. 6883 feet) The Huck Fire, which started near here when wind blew a tree onto a power line, burned 20,000 park acres and forced the evacuation of South Entrance residences in July 1988.

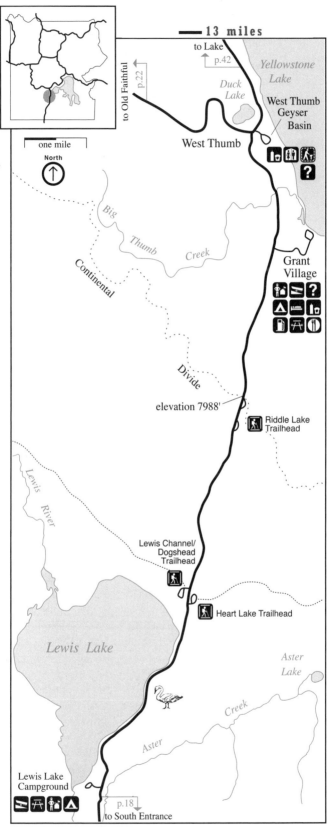

to Old Faithful p.22

to Lake
p.42

13 miles

*Yellowstone
Lake*

*Duck
Lake*

West Thumb
Geyser
Basin

West Thumb

Big

Thumb

Creek

Continental

Grant
Village

Divide

elevation 7988'

Riddle Lake
Trailhead

*Lewis
River*

Lewis Channel/
Dogshead
Trailhead

Heart Lake Trailhead

Lewis Lake

*Aster
Lake*

Creek

Aster

Lewis Lake
Campground

p.18
to South Entrance

one mile

North
↑

West Thumb Bay: The view to the east is across the widest part of Yellowstone Lake—18 miles to Steamboat Point. West Thumb Bay occupies the flooded crater left by a large volcanic eruption 125,000 to 200,000 years ago, similar to the great caldera eruption—600,000 years ago.

West Thumb Geyser Basin: One of the smaller geyser basins in Yellowstone, West Thumb is an interesting and scenic basin because of its location along the lake. A stone mantle, a mile long and in places 18 feet thick, has been deposited by hot springs along the shore.

The basin offers a variety of colorful hot springs, mud pots, pools, fumaroles, and geysers. Its most famous attraction, Fishing Cone, is a shoreline geyser that protrudes from the lake bottom. Early tourists claimed you could catch a trout from the lake, and without moving a step you could dip it into the boiling waters of Fishing Cone and cook it on the hook. This amusement is now forbidden by park regulations.

Grant Village: This recent park development was constructed in the late 1970s on the shore of Yellowstone Lake. The area was evacuated when the forest fires known as the Snake River Complex threatened in July 1988. The visitor center features a museum display telling the story of fires in Yellowstone.

Continental Divide: (Elev. 7988 feet) All water falling to the south of the divide flows via the Snake and Columbia Rivers to the Pacific Ocean; all water to the north eventually reaches the Atlantic Ocean. The Continental Divide meanders for about 115 miles across the high, rolling plateau country of central Yellowstone. In the park the divide follows no razor's edge and is often difficult to discern.

Lewis Lake: The highway parallels the east shore of the lake for 2.5 miles. Lewis, 108 feet deep and the third largest lake in Yellowstone, is connected to Shoshone Lake by a narrow channel famous for its brown trout fishing. Browns are not native to Yellowstone. They were introduced, along with brook, rainbow, and lake trout in the early years of the park before biologists recognized that exotic fish would compete with native cutthroat trout. Park managers might wish the foreign species gone, but fishermen look forward each autumn to the annual run of Lewis Lake browns to Shoshone Lake.

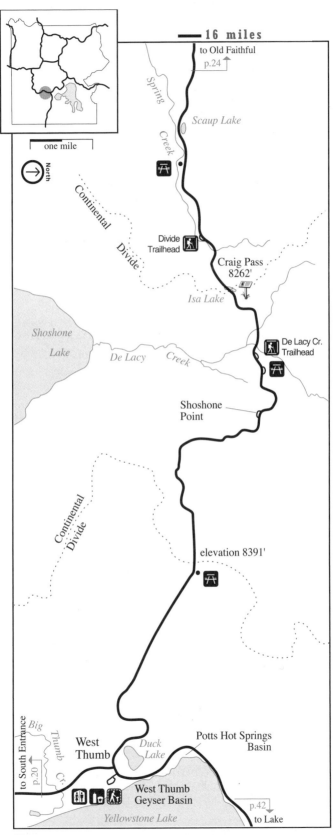

16 miles

to Old Faithful
p.24

Spring Creek

Scaup Lake

Continental Divide

Divide Trailhead

Craig Pass 8262'

Isa Lake

Shoshone Lake

De Lacy Creek

De Lacy Cr. Trailhead

Shoshone Point

Continental Divide

elevation 8391'

one mile

North

Big Thumb Cr.

to South Entrance
p.20

West Thumb

Duck Lake

Potts Hot Springs Basin

West Thumb Geyser Basin

p.42
to Lake

Yellowstone Lake

West Thumb to Madison

Scaup Lake: Near here, in August 1908, at a place then called Turtle Rock, the biggest stagecoach robbery of the 20th century occurred—$2,000 was stolen. Not much in terms of today's dollar, but a lot of money when a cowboy earned a few dollars a month. The robber eluded capture. This holdup was one of five in Yellowstone.

Craig Pass and Isa Lake: This pass straddles the Continental Divide (elev. 8262 feet). Isa Lake has two outlets; because the divide twists on itself, the western outlet flows to the Atlantic Ocean and the eastern outlet to the Pacific.

De Lacy Creek: The creek was named for a prospector, Walter Washington DeLacey, who passed this way in 1863, when reports of Yellowstone's wonders were still tall tales, considered too strange to be true.

Shoshone Point: The point overlooks, in the distance, the park's second largest lake. Shoshone Lake was named for the Idaho tribe. A geyser basin lies on the remote far shore of the lake. On the old wagon road near here, in July 1914, a convoy of 15 stagecoaches was robbed, one coach after the other, at rifle point. The lone bandit, who netted about $1,000, was a poacher from Idaho named Edward B. Trafton. No novice, he had previously been convicted of robbing his mother-in-law. This time he was also caught (having been photographed and sketched by tourists).

Continental Divide: (Elev. 8391 feet) The divide is like the peak of the roof of the continent, splitting the waters to flow toward the opposite coasts of North America.

Duck Lake: The lake occupies a steam explosion crater made some 10,000 years ago when a glacial ice dam gave way, suddenly draining a deep lake above a group of hot springs. The underlying superheated water flashed to steam, causing a mighty explosion.

Yellowstone Lake: This cold and clear lake can be like a vast mirror, doubling the big sky and the fleecy clouds above; then, rising afternoon winds can transform it to a whitecapped, gray, and sometimes deadly wilderness. On the far horizon, the Absaroka Mountain Range, a chain of volcanoes that were active about 50 million years ago, marks the park's eastern boundary.

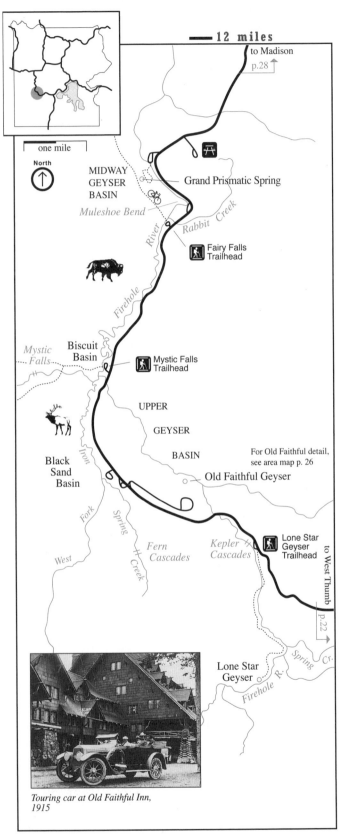

to Madison
p.28

one mile

North
↑

MIDWAY
GEYSER
BASIN

Grand Prismatic Spring

Muleshoe Bend

Rabbit Creek

Fairy Falls
Trailhead

Firehole River

Mystic Falls

Biscuit
Basin

Mystic Falls
Trailhead

UPPER

GEYSER

BASIN

For Old Faithful detail,
see area map p. 26

Black
Sand
Basin

Old Faithful Geyser

Iron Spring Creek

West Fork

Fern Cascades

Kepler Cascades

Lone Star
Geyser
Trailhead

to West Thumb
p.22

Lone Star
Geyser

Firehole R.

Spring Cr.

*Touring car at Old Faithful Inn,
1915*

24

Midway Geyser Basin: Here a boardwalk leads to Excelsior Geyser, one of the world's biggest. During the 1880s it erupted to a height of 300 feet. It erupted again in 1985 but only to a height of 80 feet. Beyond this gaping 300-foot-wide crater is Grand Prismatic Spring, the largest hot spring in Yellowstone and second largest in the world, well named for its colorful bands of yellow, red, and green thermal algae.

At Muleshoe Bend, the road overlooks a group of very hot pools. In 1978 a man jumped in trying to rescue his dog and was severely burned. At least 13 visitors have died in Yellowstone hot springs since the park's establishment in 1872. Some hot springs are surrounded by overhanging shelves of mineral deposits that can break off without warning. The bones of elk and bison at the bottom of several pools attest to that fact.

Rabbit Creek is fed by the runoff from a group of backcountry hot springs.

Biscuit Basin: It was named for mineral deposits around the fringe of Sapphire Pool. Most were destroyed by violent eruptions triggered by the 1959 Yellowstone earthquake (7.1 on the Richter scale). Mystic Falls Trail leads 1 mile to a 70-foot-high chain of cascades.

Firehole River: Firehole is one of the oldest names in Yellowstone. Fur trappers used "hole" for valley. Fire refers not only to the abundant steaming hot springs along the river, but also to the effects of a big forest fire that burned the area around 1800, a few years before mountain men first entered Yellowstone.

Black Sand Basin: The basin includes a readily accessible cluster of especially colorful hot springs and geysers. The sand for which the area is named is made of obsidian (black volcanic glass) formed when lava encountered ice and suddenly chilled. A short boardwalk crosses Iron Spring Creek, a beautiful little stream that bisects the basin.

Upper Geyser Basin: (Elev. 7341 feet) Basins are formed in Yellowstone where glacial sand and gravel have accumulated in low places between vast mounds of lava. The Upper Basin contains the most extraordinary concentration of hydrothermal phenomena in the world—more than 70 geysers, including Old Faithful and more than 600 other hot springs and steam vents.

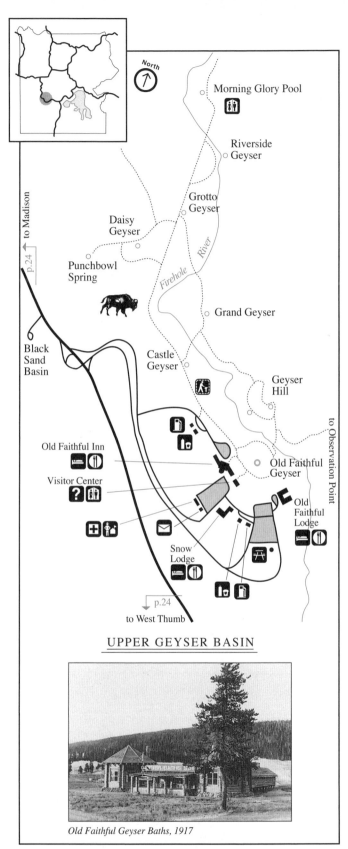

Morning Glory Pool

Riverside Geyser

Grotto Geyser

Daisy Geyser

Punchbowl Spring

Firehole River

to Madison

p.24

Black Sand Basin

Grand Geyser

Castle Geyser

Geyser Hill

Old Faithful Inn

Visitor Center

Old Faithful Geyser

to Observation Point

Old Faithful Lodge

Snow Lodge

p.24

to West Thumb

UPPER GEYSER BASIN

Old Faithful Geyser Baths, 1917

Old Faithful Area

Old Faithful Area Upper–Geyser Basin: Stretching for 2 miles along the Firehole River, the Upper Geyser Basin contains about a quarter of the world's geysers. In America's arid West a cold spring—water springing out of the earth—seems something of a miracle. In this basin water flows or blows out of the ground in hundreds of places. The wonder of it is quite extraordinary.

Trails and Boardwalks: Trails through the basin will take hikers past many notable and interesting geysers, including Castle Geyser, which may be the oldest geyser in Yellowstone. Castle erupts every nine hours to a height of 60 to 90 feet from a cone 12 feet high. Also here are Grotto Geyser, whose vent cone has engulfed a group of trees creating bizarre shapes, and Riverside Geyser, whose eruptions every seven hours (one of the most regular in the park) throw hot water in an arch over the Firehole River. The basin includes about 75 active geysers and at least 600 significant hot springs.

Old Faithful Geyser: This national icon and the world's most famous geyser erupts more frequently than the other big geysers in the basin, although it is neither the largest nor the most regular geyser. Eruption intervals vary from 35 to 120 minutes, but usually fall between 65 and 92 minutes. Eruptions last from 2 to 5 minutes and reach a height of 90 to 184 feet, emitting 10,000 to 12,000 gallons of water. Named by the Washburn Expedition, in early years the geyser was abused by visitors stuffing its vent with logs, boulders, and junk for the amusement of watching the debris blow out.

Yellowstone's myriad geothermal features are nourished by meltwater from the average 250 inches of snow during a typical winter. Seeping through cracks in the lava rocks, and accumulating in subterranean spaces, the water encounters deep heat rising from molten magma far below. The heat powers the underground circulation of water and reveals itself as hot springs and geysers.

Old Faithful Inn: Built during the winter of 1903–04, this old, distinguished hotel is said to be the largest log structure in the world; the lobby ceiling is 84 feet high. Constructed from local materials, with much of its hardware made on the spot by blacksmiths, the inn is a masterwork of stone and log construction—rustic, organic, and in harmony with its wild setting.

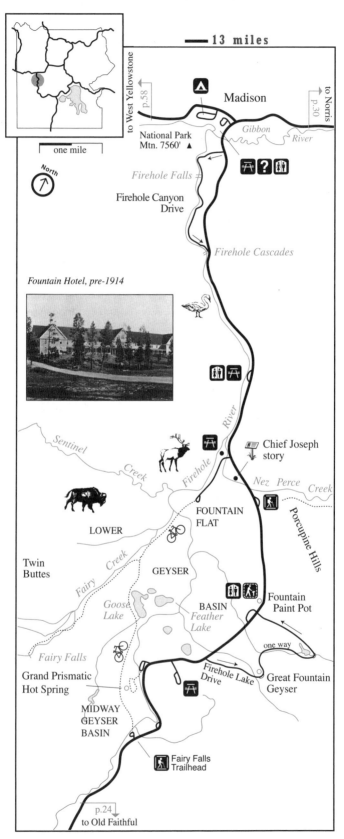

━━ 13 miles

to West Yellowstone → p.58

to Norris → p.30

Madison

National Park
Mtn. 7560' ▲

Gibbon River

Firehole Falls

Firehole Canyon
Drive

Firehole Cascades

Fountain Hotel, pre-1914

Sentinel Creek

Firehole River

Chief Joseph
story

Nez Perce Creek

FOUNTAIN
FLAT

LOWER

Twin
Buttes

Fairy Creek

GEYSER

Goose Lake

BASIN

Feather Lake

Porcupine Hills

Fountain
Paint Pot

Fairy Falls

Grand Prismatic
Hot Spring

Firehole Lake
Drive

one way

Great Fountain
Geyser

MIDWAY
GEYSER
BASIN

Fairy Falls
Trailhead

p.24
to Old Faithful

one mile

North

28

Firehole Canyon Drive: The one-way road (once the main highway) passes along 800-foot-high lava cliffs. The road climbs along the canyon wall past the 40-foot-high Firehole Falls and the Cascades of the Firehole. The Firehole River is one of the world's classic trout streams, though some stretches are so warmed by hot springs that they are avoided by fish.

Fountain Flat: Near the Nez Perce picnic area, surrounded by an iron railing, is the grave of Mattie Culver, a winterkeeper's wife who died at the old Fountain Hotel in 1889. From the road's end, a foot and bicycle trail leads to Ojo Caliente, a fine example of a crested hot spring. Beyond lies Goose Lake, a pleasant place to picnic, and a foot trail to 200-foot-high Fairy Falls.

Nez Perce Creek: This creek is named for Chief Joseph's tribe ("the pierced noses") who passed this way during the summer of 1877. Having been ordered to a reservation in Oregon, they chose instead to flee, the U.S. Army on their heels, to northern Montana, where they were stopped a few miles short of the Canadian border.

Twin Buttes and Porcupine Hills: To the west and east, respectively, these hills are piles of rocks and gravel released from the ice that melted when glaciers passed over groups of hot springs. The Twin Buttes were burned by the North Fork Fire, the largest (406,000 acres) of the 1988 fires.

Fountain Paint Pot: A short boardwalk leads to a group of oxide-colored mud pots—pools of hot clay entertaining for their blooping and spitting. Also here are several constantly erupting geysers, including Clepsydra, a fine sight at sunset.

Firehole Lake Drive: Opposite the drive's entrance stand lodgepole pines killed by hot spring runoff. By capillary action the dead trees have soaked up mineral-laden water, which colors their bases white and retards decay. These skeletons have stood here for decades.

The drive passes several superb geysers and hot springs. The largest, Great Fountain Geyser, is one of the grand geysers of the world, erupting every 8 to 12 hours. Just beyond, White Dome Geyser sports a massive cone and erupts every 12 to 24 minutes in a jet of water that turns to steam and spray.

to Mammoth   p.44

to Canyon   p.32

Norris Campground

■ museum

Norris Geyser Basin

Norris

Steamboat Geyser

Gibbon Hill
▲ 8601'

ELK

PARK

rapids

MEADOWS

Chocolate Pots ○

Geyser   *Creek*

GIBBON

Gibbon Meadows
Picnic Area

Artist
Paintpots

Sylvan Springs ○ ○ ○

Gibbon

Canyon

Beryl Spring ○

one way

Iron Spring ○

landslides area

Gibbon Falls 84'

River

Tuff Cliff
Picnic Area

Gibbon

Terrace Spring ○

Madison

↓ p.58

p.28 ↓

to West Yellowstone

to Old Faithful

one mile

North

Madison to Norris

Norris Geyser Basin: (Elev. 7484 feet) Named for Yellowstone's second superintendent, Norris is the hottest, most active geyser basin in the park. Underground water temperatures of 706°F have been measured. The Norris Museum, built in 1930 of massive logs and native stone by the Civilian Conservation Corps, is a classic example of park architecture. Two loop trails pass through the basin. The Back Basin Trail (1.5 miles) passes Steamboat Geyser, the highest-erupting (380 feet) active geyser in the world.

Chocolate Pots: Located along the banks of the Gibbon, where boulders stand on pedestals in the river, these 3- to 4-foot warm-spring mounds are composed of mineral-cemented iron oxides, aluminum, manganese, and nickel, and are further colored by algae.

Gibbon Meadows: Six groups of geysers and springs are located in the basin. Artist Paint Pots are accessible by a side road at the south end of the basin. To the east, Gibbon Hill rises more than 1,000 feet above the basin floor and is so symmetrical that in satellite photos it looks man-made. The Sylvan Springs group is located across the Gibbon River on the west side of the basin. The basin meadows host year-round herds of elk and bison. The huge North Fork Fire, which cut a wide swath more than 50 miles long, passed through here on its way northeast in August 1988.

Beryl Spring: Beryl Spring, one of the hottest in the park, takes its name from the blue-green gemstone.

Gibbon Falls: The 84-foot falls were created where the Gibbon River spilled over the rim of Yellowstone's great volcanic crater that erupted 600,000 years ago. The falls have since eroded and receded a half mile upstream.

Gibbon River: This river is named for Gen. John Gibbon, who explored the area in 1872. Gibbon led the cavalry unit that buried Custer's men on the Little Bighorn, and in 1877 he helped chase Chief Joseph and the Nez Perce through the park on their desperate flight for refuge in Canada.

Terrace Spring: Mineral deposits have formed terraces along the runoff channels of this spring. Nearby, yellow monkey flowers bloom for much of the year.

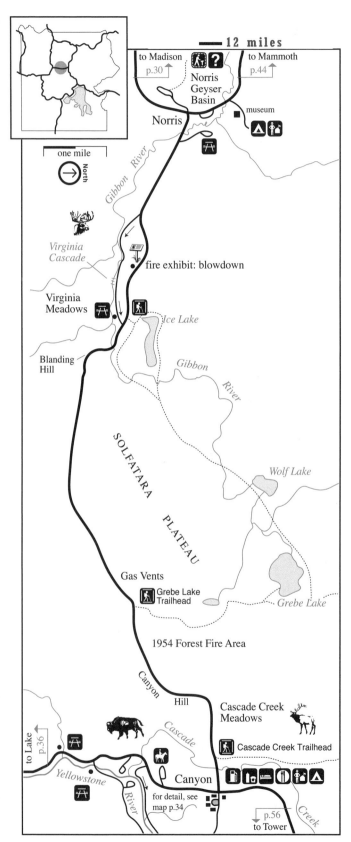

to Madison
p.30

to Mammoth
p.44

Norris
Geyser
Basin

museum

Norris

━━━ 12 miles

one mile

North

Gibbon River

*Virginia
Cascade*

fire exhibit: blowdown

Virginia
Meadows

Ice Lake

Blanding
Hill

Gibbon

River

Wolf Lake

SOLFATARA

PLATEAU

Gas Vents

Grebe Lake
Trailhead

Grebe Lake

1954 Forest Fire Area

Canyon
Hill

Cascade

Cascade Creek
Meadows

Cascade Creek Trailhead

to Lake
p.36

Yellowstone

River

Canyon

for detail, see
map p.34

p.56
to Tower

Creek

32

Norris to Canyon

Norris Area Meadows: Hot springs make these meadows year-round elk range. The Museum of the National Park Ranger, at the campground, is worth a visit.

Virginia Cascade: A one-way, 3-mile-long road follows a spectacular stretch of river where the Gibbon tumbles down off the Solfatara Plateau creating the 60-foot-high Virginia Cascade. The idyllic willow meadows above the cascade sometimes host moose.

Gallatin Mountain Range: Prominent as the western boundary of the park, the range was named by Lewis and Clark in 1805 for Albert Gallatin, President Thomas Jefferson's Secretary of the Treasury.

Fire Exhibit—Blowdown: This roadside burn is one of the most dramatic in the park. During the summer of 1984 a mountain tornado blew down tens of thousands of lodgepole pines along its 22-mile path, which crossed the road here. Over the course of the next four summers the logs became tinder dry, fueling an extremely hot burn during the 1988 North Fork Fire. Generally not moist, this area may be a long time in regeneration.

Blanding Hill: Here the highway climbs the west slope of the Solfatara Plateau, about 12 miles wide and 700 feet high, formed by one of the outpourings of viscous lava that followed the collapse of the Yellowstone caldera 600,000 years ago. Solfatara means "gas vent." The lack of water on the plateau keeps the Solfatara geothermal area dry—hot and steamy on cool mornings, but devoid of springs or geysers.

Old Forest Fire Burn: This former burn offers a preview of how Yellowstone will appear in the future as the park regenerates from the 1988 fires. Although most of the plateau is covered by lodgepole pine, stands of old spruce and fir grow on the slopes of Canyon Hill to the east—a sign of better soil and more moisture.

Cascade Creek Meadows: One lobe of the North Fork Fire passed a quarter of a mile north of here before running over the Washburn Range and continuing to burn for another 25 miles to the northeast.

Cascade Creek begins at Cascade Lake, a mile to the northwest. Beaver, moose, and grizzly bears frequent the meadows.

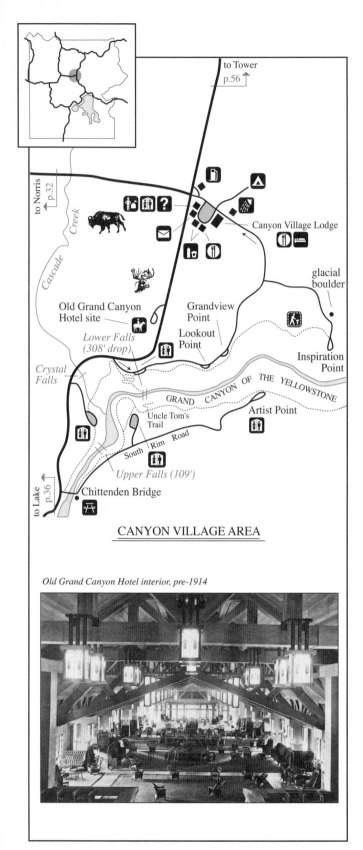

to Tower
p.56

to Norris p.32

Cascade Creek

Canyon Village Lodge

glacial boulder

Old Grand Canyon Hotel site

Grandview Point

Lookout Point

Lower Falls (308' drop)

Inspiration Point

Crystal Falls

GRAND CANYON OF THE YELLOWSTONE

Artist Point

Uncle Tom's Trail

South Rim Road

Upper Falls (109')

to Lake p.36

Chittenden Bridge

CANYON VILLAGE AREA

Old Grand Canyon Hotel interior, pre-1914

Canyon Village Area

Canyon Area—North Rim Road: Here on Inspiration Point Road, a large glacial boulder, estimated to weigh 500 tons, lies 15 miles from the nearest possible place of origin. The boulder was dropped by melting ice 10,000 years ago. Inspiration Point offers a view down canyon. Back on the rim road, Grandview Point looks downriver to where the colorful canyon is widest. Lookout Point provides the classic north rim view of the Lower Falls (308 feet). At high water, during the spring snow melt, 64,000 gallons per second pass over these falls. At low water the flow diminishes to about 5,000 gallons per second. Ospreys nest in piles of sticks perched atop rock pinnacles in the canyon.

Upper Falls: This spectacular falls is called "Upper" because it is upstream of the Lower Falls. Confused? Try this one: the Upper Falls (109 feet) is the lower falls and the Lower Falls (308 feet) is the higher falls. The Upper Falls was formed where a hard lava flow abuts a soft one. In 1880 a tree nearby was discovered with the initials "JOR" and the date "Aug 19, 1819" carved on it. A short trail begins at the parking area and leads to the 129-foot-high Crystal Falls of Cascade Creek.

South Rim Road: Across the Chittenden Bridge (named for Hiram Chittenden, the pioneer park highway engineer and first historian of the park) this 2.5-mile dead-end drive passes along the south rim of the Grand Canyon of the Yellowstone. Here, Uncle Toms Trail provides a view of the Upper Falls from near the parking lot. The trail continues down an iron stairway into the canyon for a noisy, close-up view of the Lower Falls. Artist Point an overlook a mile away offers a classic, sweeping view of the Grand Canyon and the Lower Falls.

Grand Canyon of the Yellowstone: Measuring 1,200 feet at its deepest point, 4,000 feet across, and 24 miles long, this canyon is basically a river-eroded geyser basin. Hot acidic water from numerous springs in the canyon have weakened the volcanic rocks here, making them vulnerable to rapid erosion and allowing the creation of a fast-expanding canyon. The Lower Falls is located at the transition zone between hydrothermally altered rock and rock that, being unaffected by hydrothermal alteration, remains hard. The vivid colors in the canyon come from minerals and oxides leached out of the decaying rocks by the waters.

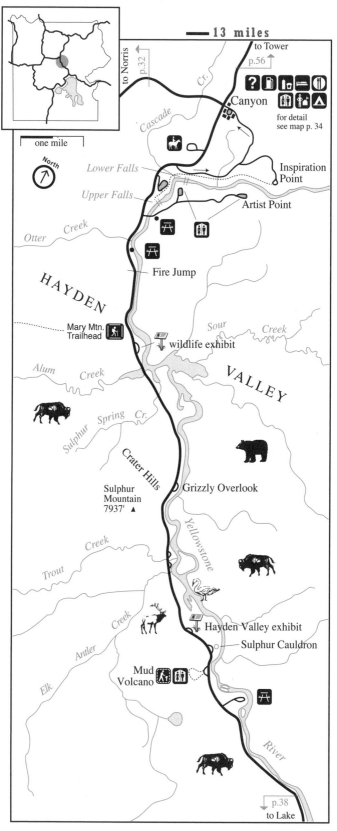

to Norris
p.32

to Tower
p.56

Canyon

for detail
see map p. 34

one mile

North

Lower Falls

Inspiration
Point

Upper Falls

Artist Point

Otter   Creek

HAYDEN

Fire Jump

Mary Mtn.
Trailhead

Sour   Creek

wildlife exhibit

Alum   Creek

VALLEY

Sulphur   Spring   Cr.

Crater Hills

Sulphur
Mountain
7937'

Grizzly Overlook

Yellowstone

Trout   Creek

Antler   Creek

Hayden Valley exhibit

Sulphur Cauldron

Mud
Volcano

Elk   Creek

River

p.38
to Lake

Canyon to Lake

Canyon Village: The grove of trees beyond the pond to the west burned in September 1988, when a finger of the North Fork Fire made a run on the village and was stopped by firefighters just yards from the buildings.

Otter Creek: Tourists who camped here in the summer of 1877 were attacked by some Nez Perce warriors as Chief Joseph's people fled across the park in their bid to reach Canada. The Mount Washburn range is visible downriver to the north.

Otter Creek Picnic Area: In October 1987, a photographer was killed by a five-year-old sow grizzly bear in the meadows west. Here, the North Fork Fire jumped across the Yellowstone via the timbered ridge on the south side of these meadows. The 1988 fires sometimes cast burning embers 2 miles ahead. Thus, with strong winds, the fires moved as much as 13 miles a day, consuming huge tracts of forest in a few hours.

Yellowstone River: A 1797 map gave the river a French name, *R. des Roches Jaune*, "river of the yellow rocks." The name probably referred to rocks near the river's junction with the Missouri River near the Montana–North Dakota border. Measuring 675 free-flowing miles from its source to its mouth, the Yellowstone is the longest undammed river in the lower 48.

Hayden Valley: Ferdinand V. Hayden was a pioneer surveyor who led an expedition to Yellowstone in 1871. He was instrumental in the creation of the park. This was the site of a fur trapper's mini-rendezvous in 1836 led by mountain man "Chief" Jim Bridger.

In Hayden Valley, Alum Creek was named for its astringent taste, caused by minerals leached into it by upstream hot springs. An early tall tale claimed that its mouth-puckering water would shrink the hooves off any animal that forded the creek. Sulphur Spring Creek flows from the twin Crater Hills to the west. The hills are glacial moraines built of rocks and gravel dropped by the ice melting as it came into contact with the hot springs. The hills are cemented by hot springs minerals. In 1985 a Park Service naturalist and her husband were severely mauled in these hills when they surprised a sow grizzly with two cubs feeding on a bison carcass. Mount Washburn, with the lookout tower on its summit, is clearly visible to the northeast.

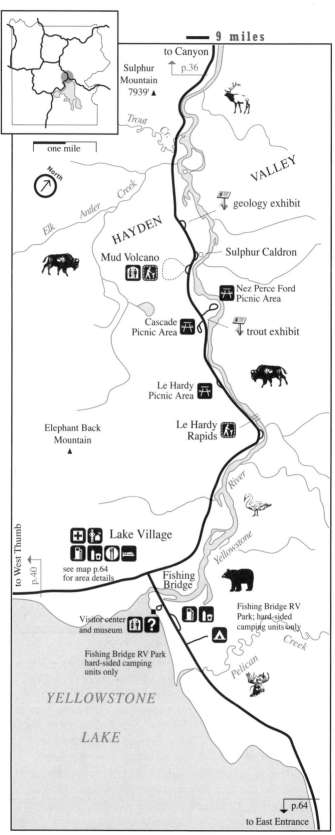

9 miles

to Canyon

p.36

Sulphur
Mountain
7939' ▲

Trout Cr.

one mile

North

VALLEY

geology exhibit

HAYDEN

Sulphur Caldron

Elk   Antler   Creek

Mud Volcano

Nez Perce Ford
Picnic Area

Cascade
Picnic Area

trout exhibit

Le Hardy
Picnic Area

Elephant Back
Mountain
▲

Le Hardy
Rapids

River

Lake Village

Yellowstone

see map p.64
for area details

Fishing
Bridge

to West Thumb

p.40

Fishing Bridge RV
Park; hard-sided
camping units only

Visitor center
and museum

Fishing Bridge RV Park
hard-sided camping
units only

Pelican   Creek

YELLOWSTONE

LAKE

p.64

to East Entrance

Trout Creek: The creek flows from the west in graceful meanders amid cutbanks of sand, silt, and clay deposited on the bottom of the old glacial lake that used to fill this valley. Avalanche Peak, in the Absaroka Range on the east boundary of the park, is the prominent, wide-faced mountain to the south.

Elk Antler Creek: Moist sedge and grass bottomlands provide good grazing for bison in winter. Sedges and grasses, which capture the energy of the sun and convert it into nourishment for plant eaters who are themselves preyed upon by carnivores, are the foundation of Yellowstone's food pyramid.

Hayden Valley: Hayden was formed 10,000 years ago when melting glacial ice 3,000 feet thick created a lake larger than today's Lake Yellowstone. The tree line around the perimeter of the valley marks that ancient shoreline. The open meadows are dotted by sagebrush. The valley, 9 miles long and 6 miles wide, is the year-round home for nearly a thousand bison; elk and grizzly bears likewise frequent the valley.

Sulphur Caldron: The stone-walled overlook to the east of the road was rebuilt in 1984 after it collapsed into the acidic pool below. The corrosive vapors rotted the foundation of the overlook. The pool has a pH nearly that of battery acid. The caldron's yellow color is caused by bacteria living in the pool.

Mud Volcano: Described and named by the 1870 Washburn Expedition, these acidic hot springs have reduced the underlying lava rock to a fine clay, producing a variety of boiling mud pools, mud pots, and mud volcanoes; a boardwalk trail leads through the best of them. The Yellowstone River bisects this thermal area, so some hot springs bubble up from the river bottom. The odor of rotten eggs, often noticeable even inside a moving car, is hydrogen sulfide gas. The ground here is warm enough that in winter most snow melts shortly after it falls, making this a good wintering area for bison.

Le Hardy Rapids: A boardwalk leads to the river where cutthroat trout jump their way upstream through this stretch of white water during the early summer spawning season. These rapids were named for the surveyor whose raft upset here in 1873.

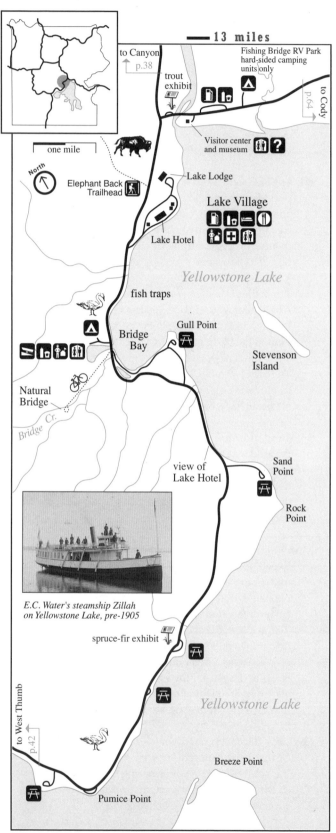

13 miles

to Canyon
p.38

trout exhibit

Fishing Bridge RV Park
hard-sided camping
units only

to Cody
p.64

Visitor center
and museum

Lake Lodge

Lake Village

Elephant Back
Trailhead

Lake Hotel

Yellowstone Lake

fish traps

North

one mile

Gull Point

Bridge
Bay

Stevenson
Island

Natural
Bridge

Bridge Cr.

view of
Lake Hotel

Sand
Point

Rock
Point

*E.C. Water's steamship Zillah
on Yellowstone Lake, pre-1905*

spruce-fir exhibit

Yellowstone Lake

to West Thumb
p.42

Breeze Point

Pumice Point

Lake to West Thumb

Lake Village: (Elev. 7744 feet) Lake Hotel, built in the
1880s to serve stagecoach visitors, is the oldest in the
park. The window-surrounded lounges offer a sweeping view of Bridge Bay and of the often dramatic
weather. Nearby, to the east, a rustic log ranger station
built in 1923 overlooks the water.

Fish Traps: A line of rocks curving out from shore, easily
visible at low water, may have been an Indian fish trap.

Bridge Bay Marina: David Folsom, who explored the area
in 1869, described a small lake, separated from the
main lake only by a sandbar, where geese and ducks
floated on mirror-smooth waters. He wrote that he
found it to be among the most beautiful places he had
seen during his expedition. The lake has since been
dredged and now harbors the Bridge Bay Marina.

Yellowstone Lake: Measuring 20 by 14 miles, 339 feet deep
with 110 miles of shoreline, the lake freezes over in late
December and thaws in late May. The water at the
bottom of the lake remains at about 42°F year-round.
On a calm afternoon the lake is like a vast mirror, but
sudden storms often sweep the lake and many compla-
cent people have been swallowed by its chilly waters.
The lake is famous for cutthroat trout fishing.

Natural Bridge: A mile-long dead-end road leads to this
water-carved arch of rock 150 feet high spanning
Bridge Creek.

Stevenson Island: Yellowstone Lake's second largest
island lies 1.5 miles offshore to the east. The hulk of
the steam excursion ship *E. C. Waters*, built in 1905,
lies near the east side of the island, where it scuttled
and burned in 1925.

Mount Sheridan: Sheridan looms 20 miles south across
the lake. At 10,308 feet, it is the highest peak of the
Red Mountains, marking the southern boundary of the
great volcanic caldera. The Absaroka Range lies across
the lake to the east.

Spruce–Fir Exhibit: About 80 percent of the park is covered
by forest, and most of that lodgepole pine. Here, where
soil is good and moisture abundant, spruce and fir trees
have succeeded pine as the dominant species.

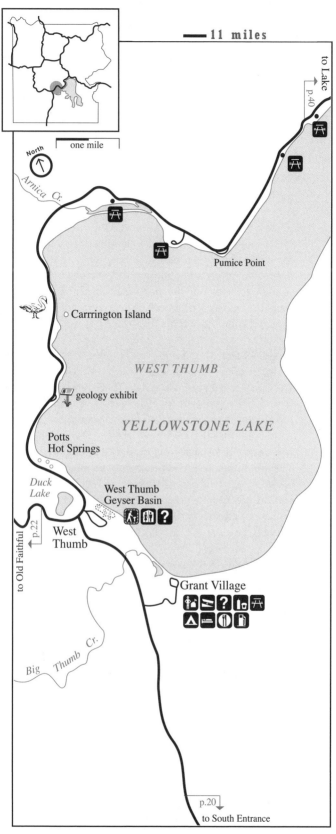

to Lake
p.40

— 11 miles

North

one mile

Arnica Cr.

Pumice Point

Carrrington Island

WEST THUMB

geology exhibit

YELLOWSTONE LAKE

Potts
Hot Springs

Duck Lake

p.22
to Old Faithful

West Thumb
Geyser Basin

West
Thumb

Grant Village

Big Thumb Cr.

p.20
to South Entrance

Pumice Point: Mount Sheridan (elev. 10,308 feet), across the lake to the south, was named for Gen. Phil Sheridan, a strong political supporter of the park in its early years. Beyond, visible on a clear day, rise the tips of the Tetons. Pumice Point marks the north-shore boundary of West Thumb Bay.

West Thumb Bay: As the deepest part of Yellowstone Lake, this large bay is a water-filled crater 4 miles across and 6 miles long. This crater was formed 200,000 years ago, some 400,000 years after formation of the great caldera. Early explorers fancied that Yellowstone Lake resembled an outspread hand and so they called this bay West Thumb.

Arnica Creek Sandbar: A wave-formed sandbar that bridges the north end of West Thumb, it was used as part of the lakeshore stagecoach road until about 1900, when a road was built on the mainland.

Carrington Island: The tiny rocky island to the east was named for a member of the Hayden Expedition of 1871.

Potts Hot Springs Basin: The basin was named for Daniel T. Potts, a fur trapper who visited the area in 1826. Some of these springs, scattered along the shore from here to the West Thumb Geyser Basin, were burned over during the summer of 1988, but the hot springs activity was unaffected by the fires.

Yellowstone Lake: With a shoreline of 110 miles and an elevation of 7,733 feet, this is one of the largest mountain lakes in North America. By late summer surface waters warm to 60°F, although the bottom remains cold.

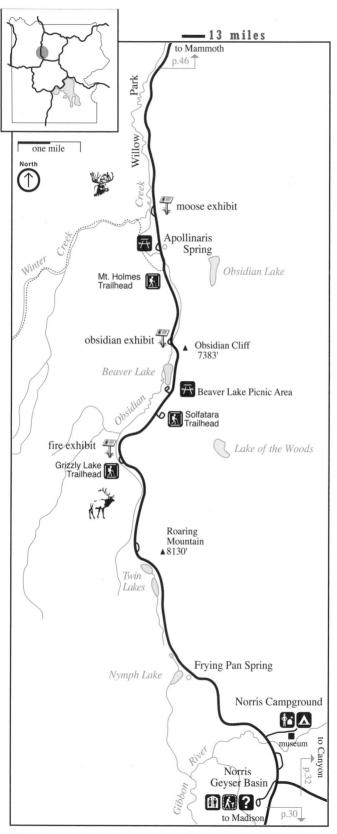

━━ 13 miles

to Mammoth
p.46

Willow

Park

Creek

Winter Creek

North

one mile

moose exhibit

Apollinaris
Spring

Obsidian Lake

Mt. Holmes
Trailhead

obsidian exhibit

▲ Obsidian Cliff
7383'

Beaver Lake

Obsidian

Beaver Lake Picnic Area

Solfatara
Trailhead

Lake of the Woods

fire exhibit

Grizzly Lake
Trailhead

Roaring
Mountain
▲8130'

*Twin
Lakes*

Frying Pan Spring

Nymph Lake

Norris Campground

museum

to Canyon
p.32

Norris
Geyser Basin

Gibbon River

to Madison
p.30

44

Norris to Gardiner

Apollinaris Spring: This water was said to resemble the 19th-century bottled mineral water, hence the name.

Obsidian Cliff: Overlooking the road to the east is Obsidian Cliff. The black volcanic glass was formed when a lava flow contacted glacial ice about 75,000 years ago. Valued by Indians for stone tools, obsidian collected here was traded as far away as the Ohio River Valley.

Beaver Lake: Extensive old beaver dams lie abandoned and overgrown. In the 1880s, when a wagon road was built through this area, a cache of beaver traps dating from the mountain man days was found nearby.

Fire Exhibit—Fire Weather: The barren hillside to the west was a centuries-old lodgepole forest until lightning caused it to burn in 1976. The huge 1988 fire, driven by high winds, engulfed and reburned this area.

Roaring Mountain: This mountain is named for the sound of steam fumaroles that became very active and noisy in 1902, killing a mountainside of trees. The activity declined in the 1920s and has been relatively quiet ever since. The acidic pool near the road is called Lemonade Pond. Ground heat and acid prevent trees from growing in much of this area.

Twin Lakes: Though separated by only a thin strip of land, the lakes are different colors. On still mornings these shallow lakes are like mirrors of the forest and sky. Both are probably without fish.

Frying Pan Spring: Shallow springs bubble with hydrogen sulphide gas that can often be smelled even in a moving car. Nearby, Nymph Lake is so acidic from hot spring activity on its bottom and shores that no fish can live in its waters.

Norris Log Soldier Station: This 1908 station, located at the campground, was used as a base for Army ski patrols. Now housing the Museum of the National Park Ranger, it is one of three soldier stations still standing in the park. (Tower and Bechler are the others.)

Norris Geyser Basin: Much of the forest around Norris burned in 1988, opening up roadside vistas and overviews of the geyser basin from the roads.

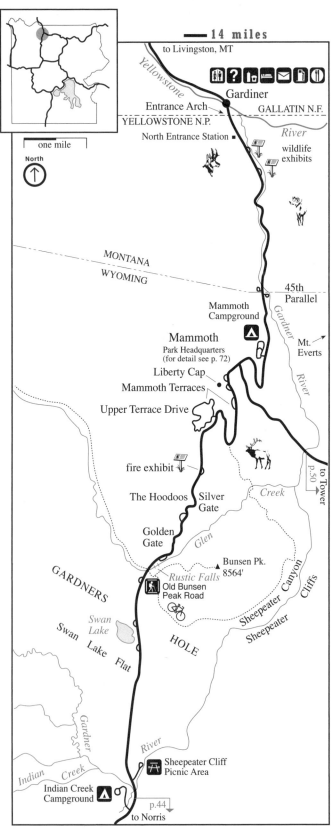

14 miles

to Livingston, MT

Gardiner

Entrance Arch

GALLATIN N.F.

YELLOWSTONE N.P.

North Entrance Station

River

wildlife exhibits

one mile

North ↑

MONTANA

WYOMING

45th Parallel

Mammoth Campground

Gardner

Mammoth
Park Headquarters
(for detail see p. 72)

Mt. Everts

Liberty Cap

Mammoth Terraces

River

Upper Terrace Drive

fire exhibit

Creek

The Hoodoos

Silver Gate

to Tower

p.50

Golden Gate

Glen

Bunsen Pk.
8564'

Rustic Falls

Old Bunsen Peak Road

GARDNERS

Sheepeater Canyon

Cliffs

Swan Lake

Sheepeater

Swan Lake Flat

HOLE

Gardner

River

Sheepeater Cliff Picnic Area

Indian Creek

Indian Creek Campground

p.44

to Norris

Theodore Roosevelt Entrance Arch: Built in 1903, the arch is inscribed "For the Benefit and Enjoyment of the People," from the 1872 Congressional act that created the park.

Mount Everts: In 1870 Truman Everts achieved dubious fame by spending 37 days lost in Yellowstone before being rescued. Five hundred dollars had been offered for the recovery of his dead body, but since he was found alive the reward was never paid. The valley's hills below the mountain are glacial moraines formed when glacial ice melted as it moved across hot springs.

Mammoth–Old Fort Yellowstone: The U.S. Army administered the park from 1886 until 1916, when the National Park Service was created. This row of stone buildings, one of which houses a visitor center, was built about 1909 as officers' quarters.

Fire Exhibit—Burn Mosaic: Fires burn unevenly depending on wind, temperature, humidity, and fuels. Hot canopy burns mingle with cool ground burns, killing some trees and leaving others untouched. The post-fire result is a greater diversity of landscape and wildlife habitat.

Golden Gate: This pass marks the north edge of Yellowstone Plateau. The highway bridge is pinned to cliffs made of crumbly volcanic yellow tuff—hence the name. Rustic Falls, 41 feet high, occupies the cleft between Bunsen Peak to the east and Terrace Mountain. Just below are The Hoodoos, a spooky jumble of boulders made of travertine—limestone deposited at the bottom of an ancient sea, then dissolved and redeposited by hot springs. Terrace Mountain has been undermined by erosion, so big blocks have broken off.

Gardners Hole: Johnson Gardner was a mountain man who frequented the area in the 1830s. Swan Lake was named for the swans that often nest there. Dominating the view to the north, 10,992-foot Electric Peak is named for the summit's storms. Bunsen Peak, 8,564 feet high, a 50-million-year-old volcanic neck, rises to the northeast.

Sheepeater Cliff: Named for a small group of Shoshone who lived here before Yellowstone became a park, the cliffs are formed of a lava flow that solidified to columnar basalt. Marmots live in burrows among the rocks.

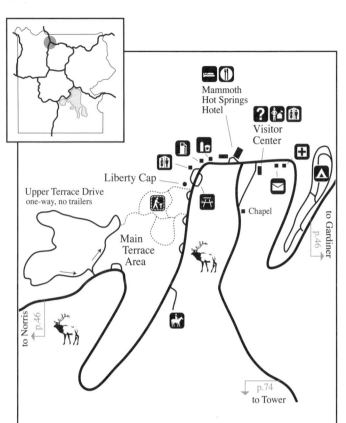

Mammoth
Hot Springs
Hotel

Visitor
Center

Liberty Cap

Upper Terrace Drive
one-way, no trailers

Main
Terrace
Area

Chapel

to Gardiner
p.46

to Norris
p.46

p.74
to Tower

MAMMOTH HOT SPRINGS AREA

*This 1923 camping arrangement featured
a combination living area and garage all in one.*

Mammoth Area

Mammoth Hot Springs—Upper Terrace Drive: This one-way, 1.5-mile road winds among large travertine terraces and mounds built by hot springs passing centuries-old juniper and offering an overview of park headquarters. Change is rapid here. Tons of minerals are deposited every day; springs rapidly seal only to reappear in new locations. The daily flow of about 750,000 gallons of hot water is steady but constantly shifting. The bright colors on active springs are produced by algae and bacteria that flourish in the water. Recent but now dry deposits are a brilliant white, while old deposits are gray. On the upper terraces beyond the road is Poison Spring, a sinkhole spring where carbon dioxide collects so densely that birds die when they come to the pond to drink. Coyotes came regularly to feed on the victims.

Main Terrace Area: Boardwalk trails wind among the ruins of both dormant and active hot springs, the new piling on top of the old like a stairway down the mountainside. The area is in a constant state of change as about two tons of travertine are deposited daily. Groundwater at about 170°F absorbs large quantities of carbon dioxide, forming carbonic acid that rapidly dissolves the underlying limestone rock. On the surface the water cools and loses some of its acidity, so lime is released and deposited as travertine. Travertine is a white mineral that, when bathed in warm water, supports a variety of colorful bacteria and algae, about 65 species of which live in Mammoth Hot Springs.

The area around Mammoth is an important part of the relatively small winter range available in the park to bison, elk, sheep, pronghorn, and mule deer. In a sense Yellowstone is large in summer and small in winter. An abundance of summer grass provides good habitat in many areas, but in winter snow makes much of the park uninhabitable and even a death trap for grazing wildlife. Traditional winter ranges, mostly north of the park boundary, were appropriated for cattle ranching during the homestead period in the late 19th century, forcing wild animals to congregate on shrunken range—including places like the post office lawn.

Mammoth Hot Springs Hotel: The third hotel on this site, it was built in the 1930s. In pre-automobile days, most visitors arrived by train at the north entrance before setting out in stagecoaches to explore the interior.

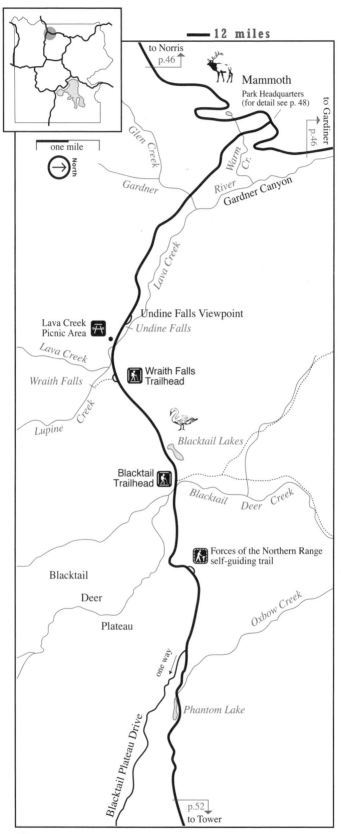

━━━ **12 miles**

to Norris
p.46

Mammoth
Park Headquarters
(for detail see p. 48)

to Gardiner
p.46

Glen Creek

Warm Cr.

Gardner River

Gardner Canyon

Lava Creek

Undine Falls Viewpoint

Lava Creek
Picnic Area

Undine Falls

Lava Creek

Wraith Falls

Wraith Falls
Trailhead

Lupine Creek

Blacktail Lakes

Blacktail
Trailhead

Blacktail Deer Creek

Forces of the Northern Range
self-guiding trail

Blacktail

Deer

Plateau

Oxbow Creek

one way

Blacktail Plateau Drive

Phantom Lake

p.52
to Tower

one mile

North

Mammoth to Tower

Warm Creek: This warm-water creek drains the terraced Mammoth Hot Springs, visible on the mountainside.

Gardner River Canyon: The deep, dark-walled canyon is visible upstream from the highway bridge. Mount Everts, which dominates the river downstream to the north, was named for a member of the 1870 Washburn Expedition who was lost in Yellowstone for 37 days, but who lived to father a son at age 76. Lava Creek Canyon lies east of the bridge.

Undine Falls: An overlook offers a fine view of the twin falls. The upper falls is 60 feet high and the lower 50 feet. The rugged mouth of Lava Creek Canyon is visible immediately downstream.

Wraith Falls of Lupine Creek: This 90-foot cascading waterfall is reached by an easy half-mile trail.

Blacktail Lakes: The meadows here burned in 1988, but the grasses quickly recovered in this normally moist ground. Since their creation by melting glaciers some of the lakes have filled in and grown over; others grow steadily smaller within a constricting grassy fringe. The Gallatin mountains dominate the west, while Bunsen Peak rises in the middle ground, 8 miles away.

Blacktail Deer Creek: Early gold miners named this creek for a Yellowstone deer that modern wildlife biologists recognize as a subspecies of mule deer.

Forces of the Northern Range Exhibit: A half-mile board-walk interprets ecological factors of Yellowstone's northern wildlife range.

Blacktail Plateau Drive: This one-way gravel road provides a pleasing 6-mile alternate to the main road. In the mid-19th century this route was used by Bannock Indians from Idaho on their annual trek to hunt buffalo (bison). Scars made by travois, the twin poles tied to horses to haul baggage or children, are still visible in places across the sagebrush grasslands. Later, the trail was improved to accommodate stagecoaches.

Phantom Lake: This pond, filled by snowmelt waters in the spring, dries up in summer. Its muddy flats sometimes offer an interesting variety of animal tracks.

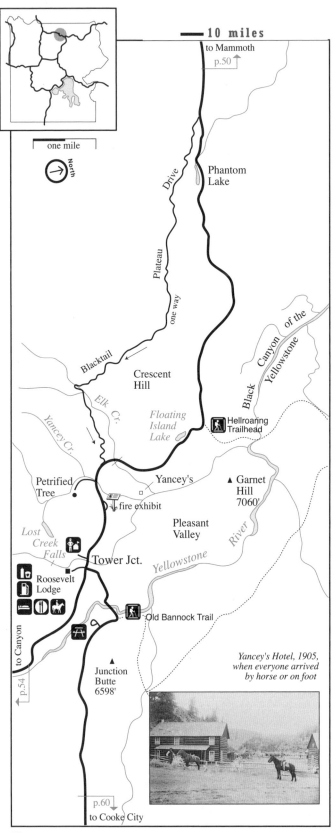

10 miles

to Mammoth
p.50

one mile

North

Plateau Drive
one way

Phantom Lake

Blacktail

Crescent Hill

Elk Cr.

Black Canyon of the Yellowstone

Yancey's Cr.

Floating Island Lake

Hellroaring Trailhead

Petrified Tree

Yancey's

▲ Garnet Hill 7060'

fire exhibit

Pleasant Valley

River

Lost Creek Falls

Tower Jct.

Yellowstone

Roosevelt Lodge

Old Bannock Trail

to Canyon
p.54

▲ Junction Butte 6598'

Yancey's Hotel, 1905, when everyone arrived by horse or on foot

to Cooke City
p.60

52

Hellroaring Mountain: To the northeast is Hellroaring Mountain, the prominent cone-shaped peak just beyond the park's boundary. Hellroaring Creek was named by a gold prospector in 1867 for the noise it made tumbling out of the mountains. The Hellroaring Fire started when an outfitter's campstove ignited his tent on August 15, 1988. The name seemed appropriate for a fire that on some days generated a convection smoke column 40,000 feet high—comparable to the cloud created by the explosion of an atom bomb.

Garnet Hill: As the name implies, this 4.5-billion-year-old granite mountain is where small, flawed garnets can be found, but not legally collected.

Yancey Creek: Around 1900, John Yancey operated a hotel nearby for stagecoach tourists and miners on their way to Cooke City, just northeast of the park.

Fire Exhibit—Winds of Change: A fierce crown fire swept this forest in 1988, giving the impression of total devastation. Yet, much of the heat of a forest fire goes upward, leaving most seeds, roots, burrowing animals, and soil microorganisms beneath the insulating earth untouched. In post-fire summers the region has produced some of the best wildflower displays in the park.

Tower Soldier Station: Near the ranger station, this is one of three surviving outposts built when Yellowstone was administered by the U.S. Army. The others are at Norris and Bechler (in the southwest corner of the park).

Petrified Tree: A half-mile side road leads to a petrified redwood tree that was buried standing alive by volcanic ash during the Absaroka Range mountain-building era some 50 million years ago. Three trees once stood on this site. Two were carried off in pieces by souvenir hunters. The other, for its protection, was enclosed by iron bars in 1907, so something of it remains to this day.

Roosevelt Lodge: (Elev. 6270 feet) President Theodore Roosevelt camped near here in 1903 before laying the cornerstone of the north entrance arch, which came to be known as the Roosevelt Arch. The rustic lodge was built in 1920 and named in memory of the President who did so much in the cause of conservation and national parks.

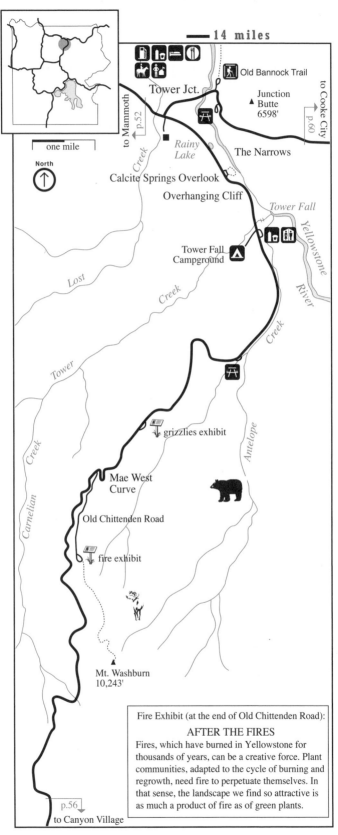

14 miles

Tower Jct.

Old Bannock Trail

Junction
▲ Butte
6598'

to Cooke City
p.60

to Mammoth
p.52

*Rainy
Lake*

Creek

The Narrows

Calcite Springs Overlook

Overhanging Cliff

Tower Fall

Tower Fall
Campground

Lost

Creek

Yellowstone

Creek

River

grizzlies exhibit

Tower

Antelope

Mae West
Curve

Creek

Old Chittenden Road

Carnelian

fire exhibit

Creek

Mt. Washburn
10,243'

Fire Exhibit (at the end of Old Chittenden Road):
AFTER THE FIRES
Fires, which have burned in Yellowstone for
thousands of years, can be a creative force. Plant
communities, adapted to the cycle of burning and
regrowth, need fire to perpetuate themselves. In
that sense, the landscape we find so attractive is
as much a product of fire as of green plants.

p.56

to Canyon Village

Tower to Canyon

Calcite Springs Overlook: A short boardwalk overlooks The Narrows—the narrowest part of the Grand Canyon of the Yellowstone River, 500 feet below. Groups of gray rock spires decorate the canyon walls and two bands of columnar basalt are graphically sandwiched between thick deposits of sedimentary gravel.

Overhanging Cliff: A lava flow of columnar basalt (like that seen from the Calcite Springs Overlook) overhangs the highway.

Tower Creek Bridge: The gray rock spires clustered below the bridge are called the Devil's Den. Tower Fall lies just below them.

Tower Fall: A short walk along the trail past the general store leads to a view of the falls. Early photographs show a large boulder precariously balanced on the brink—that boulder fell in 1986. The trail continues to the base of the falls, 132 feet high. Less than a quarter mile below, Tower Creek flows into the Yellowstone River near the old Bannock Ford, the only safe crossing of the river for many miles. The ford has been used since man first came to the Yellowstone country.

Antelope Creek: The Antelope Creek drainage is a good place to scan open meadows for elk and bears.

Mae West Curve: Named after the buxom movie star of the 1930s and '40s, the curve overlooks stands of aspen trees and the open sagebrush-grassland vistas of Antelope Creek, a favorite summer haunt of grizzly bears. Much of the area was burned over during the summer of 1988. Such meadowland fires often kill sagebrush but leave grass roots uninjured, so they grow normally, or even more vigorously the following spring, fertilized by ash leached into the soil by snowmelt. The Beartooth Mountains rise in the distance to the northeast.

Old Chittenden Road: Vehicles once drove to the top of Mount Washburn (elev. 10,243 feet). Now visitors walk the road—a rewarding 3-mile hike. The mountain was named for Gen. H. D. Washburn, who led the historic 1870 expedition through Yellowstone. Hiram Chittenden was a pioneer road engineer and Yellowstone's first historian. Look for mountain sheep and grizzly bears in the lush alpine flower meadows.

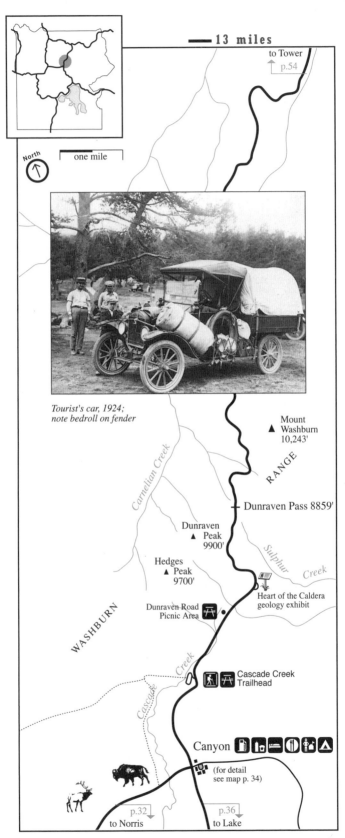

to Tower
p.54

━━ 13 miles

North
one mile

*Tourist's car, 1924;
note bedroll on fender*

Mount
▲ Washburn
10,243'

RANGE

Carnelian Creek

━ Dunraven Pass 8859'

Dunraven
▲ Peak
9900'

Sulphur Creek

Hedges
▲ Peak
9700'

Heart of the Caldera
geology exhibit

WASHBURN

Dunraven Road
Picnic Area

Cascade Creek

Cascade Creek
Trailhead

Canyon

(for detail
see map p. 34)

p.32
to Norris

p.36
to Lake

Washburn Range: The forests here were burned by a part of the North Fork Fire that came north over the Washburn Range and Canyon Village, 8 miles to the south. In such steep terrain the fires often ran very hot and fast up the mountain slopes, in a chimney effect. Other days, the fires raced down the mountains, drawn by downslope winds. Many of the 264 large mammals, mostly elk, known to have been killed by the Yellowstone fires died among the cliffs of this rugged terrain, trapped by the fast-moving fires. Almost all of the deaths were due to asphyxiation; the bodies were burned afterward.

To the north and west the road overlooks the rugged Tower Creek Canyon and beyond it to Mount Cook and Folsom Peak. Many of the trees along this stretch of highway are whitebark pines, which might take 150 seasons to produce one inch of growth rings. They bear a strongly flavored pine nut much favored by grizzly bears in the autumn. Some of the great bears hibernate on the steep north slopes of these mountains.

Dunraven Pass: (Elev. 8859 feet) The road passes between Dunraven Peak to the west, and Mount Washburn to the northeast. The pass is named for the British aristocrat, the Fourth Earl of Dunraven, who toured Yellowstone in 1874 and 1876, and whose subsequent book stimulated a wave of European travelers to visit the park.

Caldera Overlook: Stop here for an overview of the Grand Canyon of the Yellowstone, which appears at this point as a startling gash in the forested monotony of the Yellowstone interior. Beyond the canyon the roadless Mirror Plateau stretches for 15 miles to the east. The Absaroka Range, along the eastern boundary of the park, juts above the horizon far beyond. The hot springs visible from the overlook include a group of mud pots.

Grizzlies frequent the mountainous forests here throughout the summer and fall. The northern rim of the great Yellowstone caldera, which erupted 600,000 years ago, is located just to the north of here. The south side of Mount Washburn, an extinct 50-million-year-old volcano, slides into the crater created by the caldera's collapse. Mount Sheridan, visible 27 miles to the south, marks the opposite rim of this enormous geographic feature.

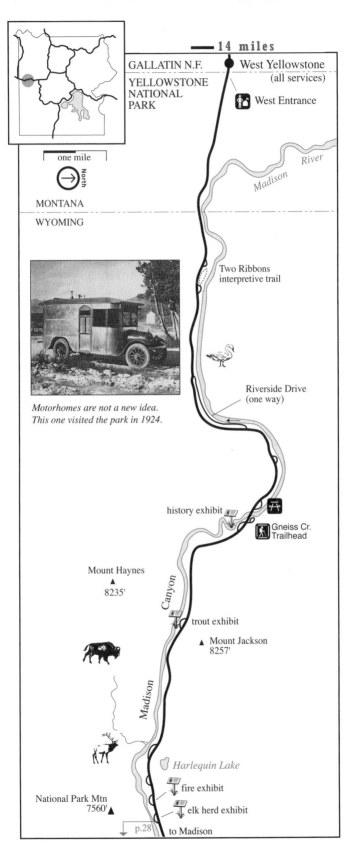

14 miles

GALLATIN N.F.

YELLOWSTONE
NATIONAL
PARK

West Yellowstone
(all services)

West Entrance

Madison River

MONTANA

WYOMING

Two Ribbons
interpretive trail

Riverside Drive
(one way)

history exhibit

Gneiss Cr.
Trailhead

Mount Haynes
▲
8235'

Canyon

trout exhibit

▲ Mount Jackson
8257'

Madison

Harlequin Lake

fire exhibit

elk herd exhibit

National Park Mtn
7560' ▲

p.28

to Madison

*Motorhomes are not a new idea.
This one visited the park in 1924.*

West Yellowstone to Madison

West Entrance: The majority of the park's roughly three million visitors enter through this gate. This boundary is dramatically visible in satellite photographs where the neighboring national forests have been clear-cut to the park line. In 1988 the North Fork Fire came within a half mile of the town of West Yellowstone.

Madison River: For centuries the Madison River was the major thoroughfare into Yellowstone—first for Stone Age hunters, then Indians, then fur trappers, explorers, and stagecoach tourists. The Madison was named by Lewis and Clark in 1805 after Secretary of State James Madison. The Madison, one of three rivers that forms the Missouri River, is considered to be one of the top trout-fishing streams in America.

Madison Canyon: The river flows between the 1,000-foot-high walls of the Madison Plateau, a former lava flow that oozed thick and viscous after the eruption and collapse of the Yellowstone caldera, 600,000 years ago. Generally, in central Yellowstone, forests cover the lava flows while meadows cover the sand and gravel left by glaciers in the low places between the flows.

Fire Exhibit—Beetle-killed and Fire-scarred: The forest here was invaded by pine bark beetles that killed many trees, providing tinder-dry wood for the 1988 blaze. Normally a dead lodgepole pine requires at least a century to rot back into the soil. A fire can return the mineral fertility to the earth in an afternoon.

Mount Haynes: This mount is named for Frank Haynes, a prominent park photographer from 1883 until his death in 1921.

Good Range: Beginning at the confluence of the Firehole and Gibbon Rivers, the Madison River Valley provides good year-round habitat for buffalo, elk, and waterfowl.

National Park Mountain: (Elev. 7560 feet) The Washburn exploration party camped near this promontory of the Madison Plateau lava flow in 1870 and, according to legend, conceived the selfless idea of a national park beside a flickering campfire. Today, historians recognize that economic motives were as important as altruism; the resulting park, however, speaks for itself.

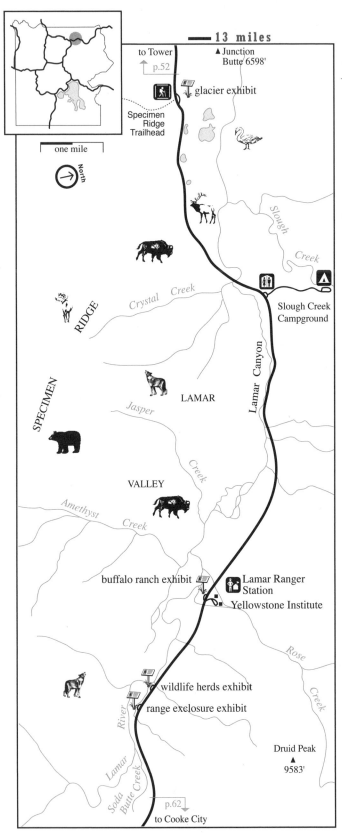

to Tower
↑ p.52

▲ Junction
Butte 6598'

glacier exhibit

Specimen
Ridge
Trailhead

one mile

North

13 miles

Slough
Creek

Slough Creek
Campground

Crystal   Creek

RIDGE

SPECIMEN

LAMAR

Jasper

Creek

VALLEY

Lamar Canyon

Amethyst

Creek

buffalo ranch exhibit

Lamar Ranger
Station
Yellowstone Institute

Rose

Creek

wildlife herds exhibit

range exclosure exhibit

Druid Peak
▲
9583'

Lamar

River

Soda

Butte Creek

p.62
to Cooke City

Tower to Northeast Entrance

Pleasant Valley: Visible to the northwest from Tower Junction, this was the site of John Yancey's hotel until 1903.

Lamar Glacier Turnout: Yellowstone has been covered by glaciers several times over the last 600,000 years; here, the lower Lamar Valley shows the results of carving by ice—glacial ponds, rolling morainal hills, and boulders dropped by melting ice. Douglas fir often grow alone in the damp shelter of the boulders. Swans nest in the ponds and bison are year-round residents of the sagebrush-grassland hills of the valley floor.

Lamar Valley: In the park's early years, the natural role of wolves and other predators was not well understood. On the contrary, predators were officially hunted, and wolves disappeared for more than 50 years. In 1996, a successful reintroduction began. Wolves now thrive in Yellowstone. Their howls echo through the Lamar Valley, and they can sometimes be seen hunting. Look for them in the early morning or evening.

Nature Note ▪ Aspen Trees: Only in the lower areas of Yellowstone is the climate temperate enough for aspens to survive. Groves of aspens sprout from common rhizomes (root masses) that may be among the longest-living things on earth. It is thought that aspens established themselves long ago in wetter, gentler times following the last ice age. Botanists believe the fires of 1988 may reinvigorate the aspens of Yellowstone. ▪

Lamar Ranger Station: This station was part of a "buffalo" ranch established in 1907 to keep the American bison from extinction. By 1902, bison had disappeared from the plains. Even in Yellowstone, poachers had reduced the herd to fewer than 40 animals. Bison were corralled for the winter near here and fed hay raised in the Lamar River bottom. The buffalo ranch ceased operations in 1952.

Specimen Ridge: The flat-topped mountain to the south entombs one of the world's most extensive fossil forests. Fifty million years ago a mature forest was buried by a deep fall of volcanic ash. Later, a second forest grew to maturity before being buried by the ash of another period. The cycle occurred 27 times; today erosion has exposed more than a hundred different fossilized species in an area of about 40 square miles.

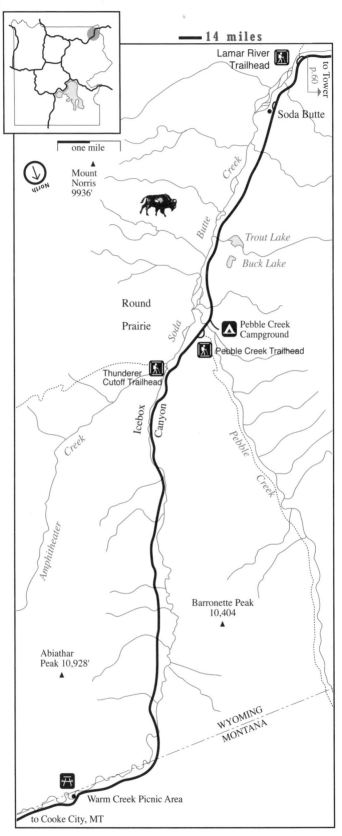

14 miles

Lamar River Trailhead

to Tower
p.60

Soda Butte

Butte Creek

Mount Norris 9936'

Trout Lake

Buck Lake

Round Prairie

Soda

Pebble Creek Campground

Pebble Creek Trailhead

Thunderer Cutoff Trailhead

Icebox Canyon

Creek

Pebble Creek

Amphitheater

Barronette Peak 10,404

Abiathar Peak 10,928'

WYOMING
MONTANA

Warm Creek Picnic Area

to Cooke City, MT

one mile

North

Soda Butte: A travertine mound formed by a hot spring, Soda Butte, today, has only a trickle of warm water flowing. Unchanged since its earliest descriptions in the 19th century, it is perhaps considered fascinating because of its isolation. No other dramatic hydrothermal feature exists nearby. On windless days Soda Butte emits a strong odor of rotten eggs. A soldier station used to stand just across the road.

Round Prairie and Pebble Creek: In the middle 1880s a man illegally built a log saloon here to serve the traffic following the trail up Soda Butte Creek to the mines around Cooke City, just beyond the park's northeast entrance. Two years later he was evicted by the Army. Had the legality of his enterprise been accepted the present-day ambience of this area would be very different. The Pebble Creek Campground is quiet (except for the noise of the stream) and generally uncrowded.

The Thunderer: Unlike most of Yellowstone, which is largely rolling high plateau country, the mountains of the northeast corner of the park are massive and dramatic. The summit of The Thunderer is a magnet for spectacular storms that are entertaining when viewed from the highway below, but fearsome close-up.

Icebox Canyon: This deep and narrow gorge cut by Soda Butte Creek is so dark and shielded from the sun that winter ice lingers long into the summer.

Barronette Peak: (Elev. 10,404 feet) This peak was named for Jack Baronette, a Scottish prospector (they misspelled his name on the first maps). The lower portion of the mountain is old limestone; the rest of it is volcanic. Barronette, with its tiers of minarets, is particularly attractive during the spring snowmelt, which creates hundreds of short-lived waterfalls on its flanks.

Nature Note ▪ Absaroka Range: Fifty million years ago a titanic period of mountain building overwhelmed the region. For ten million years a chain of volcanoes repeatedly buried thousands of square miles under lava and ash. The resulting mountain range now marks the eastern boundary of the park. The Indian tribe called by white men "Crow" called themselves Absaroka, but what the name meant to its owners has been lost. ▪

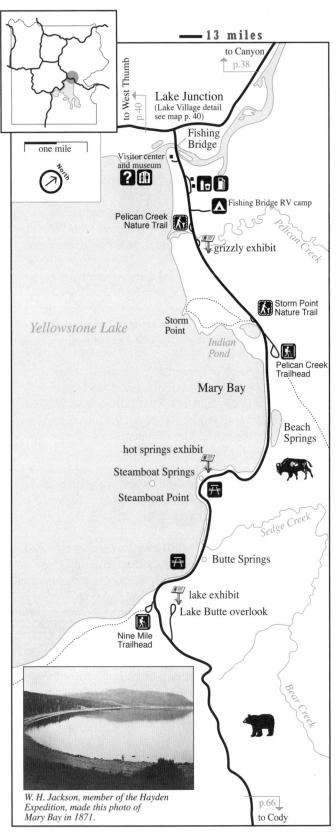

to Canyon
p.38

to West Thumb
p.40

Lake Junction
(Lake Village detail
see map p. 40)

Fishing
Bridge

Visitor center
and museum

Fishing Bridge RV camp

Pelican Creek
Nature Trail

grizzly exhibit

Pelican Creek

Storm Point
Nature Trail

Storm
Point

Indian
Pond

Pelican Creek
Trailhead

Yellowstone Lake

Mary Bay

Beach
Springs

hot springs exhibit

Steamboat Springs

Steamboat Point

Sedge Creek

Butte Springs

lake exhibit
Lake Butte overlook

Nine Mile
Trailhead

Bear Creek

one mile

North

W. H. Jackson, member of the Hayden
Expedition, made this photo of
Mary Bay in 1871.

p.66
to Cody

Lake to East Entrance

Fishing Bridge: Once a favorite fishing platform, fishing was banned in 1973 to allow the trout to spawn without disruption. Today, large cutthroat trout (named for the slashes of red below their mouths) can be seen in the crystalline water. The surrounding area is prime grizzly habitat and the history of conflict between people and bears here has become an emotional issue.

Pelican Creek: Osborne Russell, a mountain man whose memoir, *The Journal of a Trapper,* stands as a classic of the fur trade era, describes being attacked and robbed by Blackfoot Indians here in 1839. Struck by an arrow in his hip, he managed, with a wounded companion, to reach Fort Hall, more than 200 miles beyond the Tetons. Long hard walks after bad encounters with Indians were part of the mountain man's life. Those who survived had material for proud storytelling.

Indian Pond: This was a favorite Indian camping place, as evidenced by brush corrals, shelters, and discarded stone tools found here in 1880. The water-filled crater was created during the last ice age by a steam explosion. Hot springs are still active on the bottom of the pond.

Mary Bay: This large explosion crater was made when glacial ice-dammed waters suddenly drained, allowing superheated water to flash to steam. A portion of the crater's rim is marked by the semicircle of bluffs to the north. The warm ground around Beach Springs is free of snow throughout the winter. Trumpeter swans nest on nearby ponds.

Steamboat Point: The roaring steam fumarole on the lakeshore gave Steamboat Point its name. The point offers a good view of the West Thumb Geyser Basin 18 miles to the southwest. A rocky shoal named Pelican Roost Rocks lies a few hundred yards offshore.

Sedge Creek and Sedge Bay: Sedge is a grasslike plant that grows in alpine meadows and marshy river bottoms. Some varieties have a higher protein content than alfalfa.

Lake Butte: An overlook at the end of a 2-mile side road offers a grand view of the lake and its environs. On a clear day the Teton Range is visible to the south.

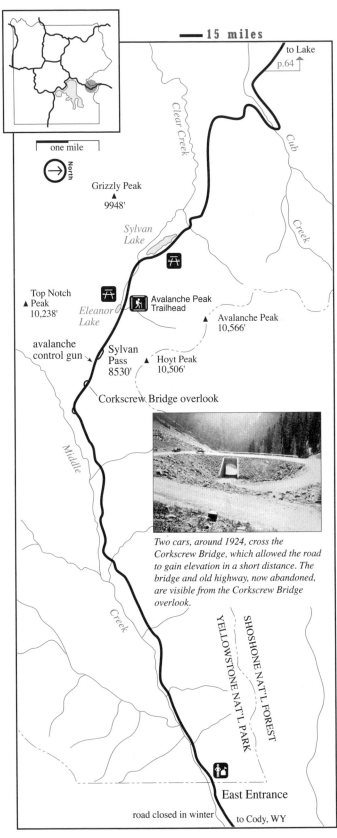

15 miles

to Lake
p.64

North
one mile

Grizzly Peak
▲
9948'

Clear Creek

Cub Creek

Sylvan Lake

Top Notch
▲ Peak
10,238'

Eleanor Lake

Avalanche Peak
Trailhead

Avalanche Peak
▲
10,566'

avalanche
control gun

Sylvan Pass
8530'

Hoyt Peak
▲
10,506'

Corkscrew Bridge overlook

Middle

Two cars, around 1924, cross the
Corkscrew Bridge, which allowed the road
to gain elevation in a short distance. The
bridge and old highway, now abandoned,
are visible from the Corkscrew Bridge
overlook.

Creek

SHOSHONE NAT'L FOREST

YELLOWSTONE NAT'L PARK

East Entrance

road closed in winter   to Cody, WY

Sylvan Lake: Sylvan means "forested, or abounding in trees." Top Notch Peak rises to 10,238 feet to the south of the lake. To the north, Avalanche Peak stands at 10,566 feet.

Eleanor Lake: Eleanor was the infant daughter of Hiram Chittenden, the pioneer highway engineer who oversaw the construction of the original road in 1902.

Sylvan Pass: (Elev. 8530 feet) This is the only park road crossing the formidable Absaroka Range, an immense chain of volcanoes 50 million years old, much more ancient than the Yellowstone Plateau. Long after most of the American West had been explored and mapped, Yellowstone remained terra incognita—remote and difficult to access within its walls of mountains. A recoilless rifled cannon is mounted on the pass in winter in order to shoot down snow cornices before they can grow large enough to avalanche. Even so, avalanches are common here.

In the summer of 1917 a teamster hauling a wagon load of hay camped near here and was fatally mauled by a large grizzly bear. The next night the same bear terrorized a nearby road camp. The crew responded by baiting a barrel with garbage and dynamite. When the griz returned they blew him up. They "raised that bear up maybe four or five feet...broke every bone in his body." The huge animal's skull measured 18 inches across the brow.

East Entrance: (Elev. 6951 feet) The frame-built ranger station was constructed in 1904 as a soldier station. Yellowstone's worst case of cabin fever—that craziness born of long winter isolation—occurred here late in the winter of 1912, when an Army sergeant returned from a ski patrol and during an altercation, shot two of his four men, killing one. He was acquitted on the grounds of self-defense. The three surviving privates, on the other hand, were found guilty of mutiny and sentenced to prison terms.

Despite the occasional case of cabin fever, isolation, and rude housing, the soldiers who served in Yellowstone generally liked being here, even in winter. Acting Superintendent Capt. George Anderson reported, "I have no difficulty in obtaining from the best of men applications for this service." Yellowstone has long been a fascination to those who visit.

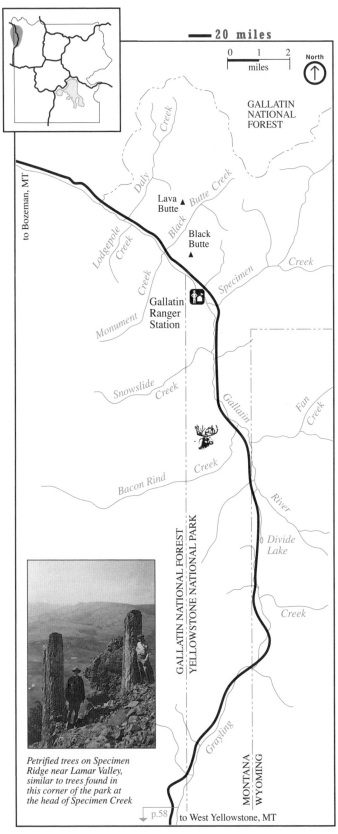

20 miles

0 1 2
miles

North
↑

GALLATIN
NATIONAL
FOREST

Daly *Creek*

to Bozeman, MT

Lodgepole *Creek*

Lava ▲
Butte

Black *Butte Creek*

Black
Butte
▲

Specimen *Creek*

Creek

Gallatin
Ranger
Station

Monument *Creek*

Snowslide *Creek*

Gallatin

Fan *Creek*

Bacon Rind *Creek*

River

Divide
Lake

Creek

GALLATIN NATIONAL FOREST
YELLOWSTONE NATIONAL PARK

Grayling

MONTANA
WYOMING

Petrified trees on Specimen Ridge near Lamar Valley, similar to trees found in this corner of the park at the head of Specimen Creek

p.58

to West Yellowstone, MT

US 191, Gallatin Valley

Gallatin River: This 20-mile stretch of highway passes in and out of the park, following the river for much of that distance. Not strictly a park road, this is the only Yellowstone highway on which visitors will encounter commercial traffic not related to park services. There is also considerable private land along this road.

The Gallatin River was named by Lewis and Clark in 1805 for the U.S. Secretary of the Treasury under President Thomas Jefferson. It was Jefferson who ordered the exploration of the vast western territory acquired by his Louisiana Purchase from France in 1803.

The trout-rich Gallatin is one of three rivers—others being the Madison and the Jefferson—that form the Missouri River near Three Forks, Montana. The Gallatin Range rises in the east, the Madison Range to the west.

Black Butte: The mountains along the highway are ancient basement rocks topped by lava laid down during the Absaroka volcanic period, 50 to 55 million years ago. Black Butte is named for is dark lava foundation.

Gallatin Ranger Station: This ranger station stands on the site of an old soldier station established here in 1910—the year this road was completed. The Army was here because in 1883 antipark forces in Congress blocked funding for Yellowstone's administration. The Secretary of the Interior, however, under authority of a bill passed three years earlier, was able to call on the Army for assistance. More accustomed to fighting Indian wars than dealing with tourists and wilderness management, the Army had a colorful and efficient tenure until the National Park Service was created in 1916.

Specimen Creek: At the headwaters stand extensive petrified forests that were buried beneath layers of volcanic ash. This area was added to the park in the 1920s to protect these fossil forests. The willows on the creek bottomland are much-favored browse of moose.

Divide Lake: On the divide between the Gallatin River and Grayling Creek is Divide Lake. Both waterways flow to the Missouri River.

Grayling Creek: Grayling are handsome native game fish, cousins of trout, sporting large, sail-like dorsal fins. Grayling are a protected species in Yellowstone.

Grand Teton: Shining Lakes and Granite Towers

A HANDFUL of the world's mountains, once seen, can never be forgotten: Europe's Matterhorn, Japan's Mount Fuji, Nepal's Ama Dablam, and Wyoming's Grand Teton, centerpiece of Grand Teton National Park. It rises, with its companion peaks, some 7,000 feet above the flat valley floor, unencumbered by foothills, gleaming with snow and ice—one of the most dramatic geologic statements on Earth.

But mountains are only part of the scene. The broad valley called Jackson Hole provides a counterpoint to the rugged crags. Winding southward from Yellowstone, the Snake River cuts a leisurely course past the Tetons on its way to Idaho and, eventually, to the Pacific Ocean. A string of lakes, shining like jewels at the base of the escarpment, occupy basins carved by glaciers. Wildlife is abundant: moose, elk, deer, bear, pronghorn, coyotes, cranes, swans, eagles, trout, and more. In summer, meadows become wildflower gardens. In fall, aspens, willows, and cottonwoods burst into color. Winter comes hard and decisively in November, bringing deep snow and exquisite, crystalline beauty.

The Tetons are among the youngest peaks in the Rocky Mountains, but they consist of very old rock that was heaved upward beginning less than ten million years ago by movement along a fault line. The western block tipped upward to create the range while the eastern block swung downward, forming the valley.

The movement continues to this day, accounting for a total displacement between the mountain block and the valley block of some 30,000 vertical feet; the valley block has fallen four times as far as the mountain block has risen. Not all of this slippage is visible because while the mountains have risen, erosion has worn them down. As evidence, a layer of sandstone on the summit of Mount Moran is a remnant of the sedimentary rock that once overlay the whole region, and which corresponds to a layer of the same sandstone now lying more than 4 miles below the valley floor.

For comparison, it is interesting to see the other side of the Teton Range, from Idaho. On the west, the range slopes more gradually, and the overlying sedimentary layers are still present. The highest peaks themselves, however, rise with the same craggy fierceness no matter from which angle they are viewed.

The human story is a short one. Indians hunted here for thousands of years, mostly during the summer, although recent evidence shows that winter camps did exist. In the early 1800s, fur trappers like John Colter, Jim Bridger, and Osborne Russell passed through looking for beaver. They never stayed long, but some of the names they used have stuck. The word "Tetons" comes from the name given to the range by French trappers: *Les Trois Tetons,* or the Three Breasts. The name makes (a little) better sense when you see the range from its more gentle western side.

The first permanent settlers were homesteaders who found that although the valley was too cold for crops, it was possible to make a marginal living raising cattle. Ranching remains a part of the local economy and the valley scene: Buckrail fences and old log barns seem to go naturally with the mountain landscape.

The park was established in 1929, more than half a century after Yellowstone. At first, it included the mountains and the morainal lakes at their base (except Jackson Lake). During the thirties, John D. Rockefeller, recognizing the future importance of preserving the area, bought up large amounts of private land in the valley. He donated that to the government in 1949 after President Franklin D. Roosevelt declared the valley floor a national monument in 1943. In 1950, Congress joined the monument and the park to form a single national park, comprising 485 square miles of mountain crag, tumbling water, and open valley.

TETON PANORAMA (As seen from near Glacier View Turnout, north of Moose Junction.)

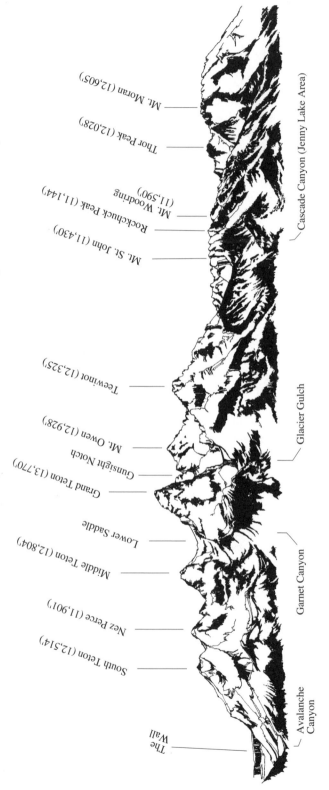

Mt. Moran (12,605')

Thor Peak (12,028')

Mt. Woodring (11,590')

Rockchuck Peak (11,144')

Mt. St. John (11,430')

Teewinot (12,325')

Mt. Owen (12,928')

Gunsight Notch

Grand Teton (13,770')

Lower Saddle

Middle Teton (12,804')

Nez Perce (11,901')

South Teton (12,514')

The Wall

Cascade Canyon (Jenny Lake Area)

Glacier Gulch

Garnet Canyon

Avalanche Canyon

■ **Mount Moran** ■ The dominant peak in the northern section of the Teton Range, Mount Moran was named for Thomas Moran, the painter who accompanied the 1871 Hayden Expedition to Yellowstone. His work was an important factor in convincing Congress to establish Yellowstone National Park in 1872, the world's first national park.

Mount Moran was first climbed by three men (Hardy, Rich, and McNulty) in July 1922, via the Skillet Glacier, a prominent long-handled glacier in the center of the east face.

■ **Teewinot Mountain** ■ Two of the first rangers in Teton Park, Fritiof Fryxell and Phil Smith, made the first ascent of this peak in 1929. The name they chose for it is a Shoshone Indian word meaning "many pinnacles," and actually might once have been the Shoshone name for the entire range.

■ **Mount Owen** ■ William Owen, an early mountaineer, had a passion to be the first on the summit of the Grand (story below).

■ **Grand Teton** ■ Wyoming has one mountain higher than the Grand Teton (Gannett Peak, in the Wind River Range), but none as spectacular. Like most of these mountains, there is no easy way up. Although any fit person with the right training or the help of a skilled guide might expect to reach the summit, getting there remains a challenging and potentially dangerous climb.

The first ascent was claimed in 1872 by Nathaniel Langford, Yellowstone National Park's first superintendent, and James Stevenson. Officially, however, by proclamation of the Wyoming State Legislature, the first successful climbers were William Owen, Bishop Spalding, John Shive, and Frank Peterson, in 1898.

Today there are dozens of routes to the top. The most popular stays close to the left-hand (south) skyline from the Lower Saddle, itself reached via Garnet Canyon and trails that originate at Lupine Meadows near Jenny Lake.

■ **The Wall** ■ At the head of Avalanche Canyon, this layer of limestone is a remnant of the sedimentary layers that once overlay the entire Teton Range, before erosion carved the mountains as we see them today.

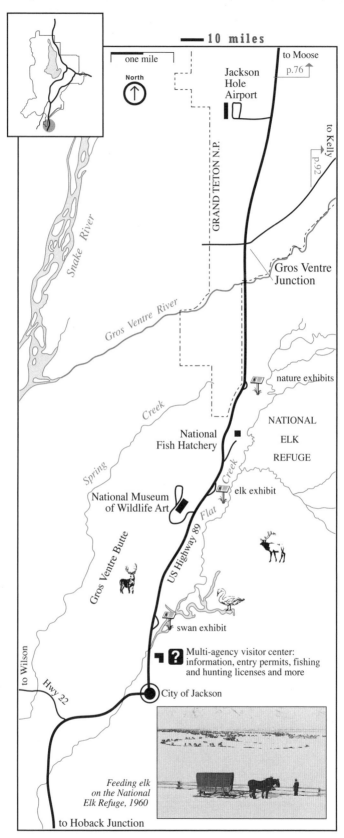

10 miles

one mile

North
↑

Jackson
Hole
Airport

to Moose
p.76

GRAND TETON N.P.

to Kelly
p.92

Gros Ventre
Junction

Snake River

Gros Ventre River

nature exhibits

Creek

National
Fish Hatchery

NATIONAL

ELK

REFUGE

Spring

National Museum
of Wildlife Art

Flat

Creek

elk exhibit

US Highway 89

Gros Ventre Butte

swan exhibit

? Multi-agency visitor center:
information, entry permits, fishing
and hunting licenses and more

to Wilson

Hwy 22

City of Jackson

*Feeding elk
on the National
Elk Refuge, 1960*

to Hoback Junction

US 89, Jackson to Moran

The Gros Ventre River: Draining the Gros Ventre Mountains to the east, this stream (pronounced GROW-vahnt) tumbles toward the Snake River. Bald eagles nest and perch in the cottonwood trees.

Grand Teton National Park Boundary: Here at the entrance, there is a fine view of the Teton Range and Jackson Hole. Fur trappers who frequented the area in the early 1800s used the word "hole" to describe a valley surrounded by mountains. William Sublette is thought to have named this valley after his partner, David Jackson, in 1829. Across the valley to the west, the cleared ski runs of Jackson Hole Ski Resort are visible on Rendezvous Mountain, just outside the park. A red tower on the summit marks the top of the aerial tram. To the south, overlooking Jackson, is Snow King Mountain, the valley's first lift-serviced ski area.

National Fish Hatchery: This facility raises cutthroat trout for Wyoming and neighboring states. Visitors are welcome from 8 a.m. to 4 p.m. Fishing access to Flat Creek is located here (fly-fishing only, August through October).

National Elk Refuge: Seven to ten thousand elk winter here each year, some coming from as far away as Yellowstone, but most from the Teton Wilderness northeast of here. The 24,700-acre refuge replaces historic wintering grounds that once stretched more than 100 miles south, to Pinedale, Wyoming, and beyond. Much of that land is now used for cattle ranching.

Driving along the refuge, look for deer on the slope to the west. Eagles, red-tailed hawks, marsh hawks, and other raptors hunt the marshy ground. To the east stands distinctively-shaped Sleeping Indian Mountain (officially Sheep Mountain) in the Gros Ventre Range.

Flat Creek: Warm springs keep Flat Creek open most of the year, attracting waterbirds like trumpeter swans and Canada geese. Sandhill cranes come through in April. Their clattering call is a sure sign of spring. Flat Creek is locally famous for its clear water and wily trout.

Town of Jackson: Services are available in Jackson. Landmarks include the famous town square with its elk-antler arches. The Jackson Hole and Greater Yellowstone Visitor Center at the north edge of town offers maps, books, permits, licenses, and more.

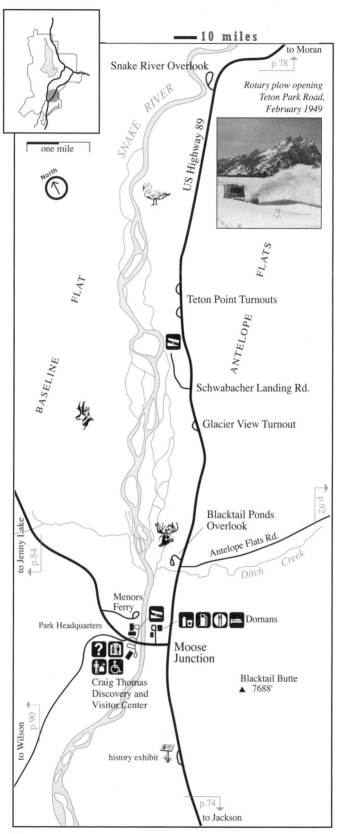

to Moran

p.78

Snake River Overlook

Rotary plow opening Teton Park Road, February 1949

SNAKE RIVER

US Highway 89

FLAT

ANTELOPE FLATS

BASELINE

Teton Point Turnouts

Schwabacher Landing Rd.

Glacier View Turnout

Blacktail Ponds Overlook

p.92

Antelope Flats Rd.

Ditch Creek

to Jenny Lake

p.84

Menors Ferry

Park Headquarters

Dornans

Moose Junction

Blacktail Butte
▲ 7688'

Craig Thomas Discovery and Visitor Center

to Wilson

p.90

history exhibit

p.74

to Jackson

one mile

North

Teton Point Turnout: This viewpoint provides a good view of the North Face of the Grand Teton. Two major peaks north of the central complex are hogbacked Mount St. John and flat-topped Mount Moran.

Schwabacher Landing Road: A 1-mile gravel road, steep and rough, goes down an old river terrace through sagebrush to moist cottonwood forest on the river bottom, and a boat landing. This is a lovely sheltered place early in the morning.

Glacier View Turnout: Stop here for a panoramic view, featuring the Teton Glacier and the gulch it carved on the northeast side of the Grand Teton. Note also the smooth Lower Saddle at the head of Garnet Canyon on the south side of the Grand. This is the most common approach for climbers attempting the Grand.

Blacktail Ponds Overlook: The Snake River's wanderings over time are apparent from the lookout perched on an old river terrace. To the north, other terraces are visible. The wetlands have developed behind beaver dams, and provide good habitat for moose and waterbirds.

Blacktail Butte: On warm days rock climbers can be seen on the smooth faces near the north end of Blacktail Butte. The routes are short but difficult. On Blacktail Butte, notice that trees grow on the north-facing sides of gullies, which receive less sun, and are cooler and wetter than south-facing slopes. The general lack of trees in Jackson Hole is explained by the cobble-filled valley soils that retain little moisture. The sagebrush flats are home to a variety of plants and animals, including pronghorn, sage grouse, rabbits, coyotes, and others. In fall watch for elk here. Looking toward the mountains, the deep gorge is Death Canyon, a popular hiking destination. To the south of it lies steeply sloped Open Canyon, followed by Granite Canyon.

Nature Note ■ Mountain Formation: The fault-block nature of the Tetons is easily seen here. You can almost imagine the mountains, riding a single vast block of stone, tipping upward to create the rampart seen today. It is more difficult to picture the valley sinking, but it has done just that, falling many thousands of feet in less than nine million years. During the ice age, glaciers eroded the mountains, filling the valley with debris. ■

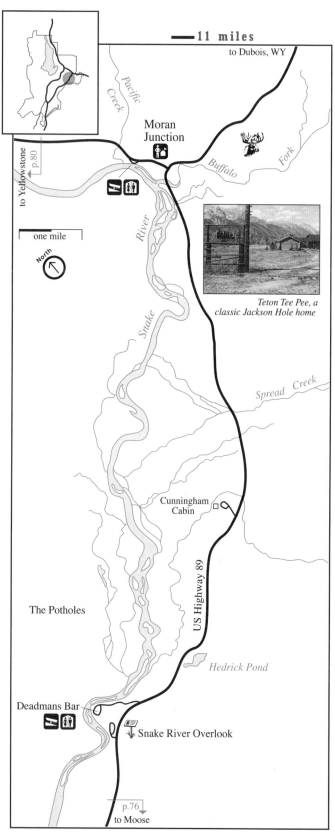

11 miles

to Dubois, WY

Pacific Creek

Moran
Junction

Buffalo Fork

to Yellowstone
p.80

River

one mile

North

Snake

Teton Tee Pee, a
classic Jackson Hole home

Spread Creek

Cunningham
Cabin

US Highway 89

The Potholes

Hedrick Pond

Deadmans Bar

Snake River Overlook

p.76
to Moose

Moran Junction: To the east is Togwotee Pass and Dubois. Go west to Yellowstone or the inner Teton Park Road.

Buffalo Fork River: Flowing out of the Absaroka Range, this river moves slowly through mixed forest and willow scrub, providing excellent habitat for moose, muskrat, and other water-loving species.

Spread Creek: Most streams flow together into one channel, but this one splits into numerous small ones, spreading out like a river delta on its way to join the Snake River a couple of miles to the west. It also spreads out upstream from here, before collecting temporarily into one stream at the bridge.

Cunningham Cabin Historic Site: J. Pierce Cunningham built a homestead here in 1890. Partially restored, it is now a historic site; pick up the self-guiding brochure.

Hedrick Pond: Barely seen through the trees to the east, this was the homestead of Charles Hedrick, who came to the valley in 1896 and became famous for the beard he grew to hide the scars from a grizzly attack.

Deadmans Bar Boat Ramp: A steep road leads to a broad river bottom named for three German prospectors allegedly murdered here in 1886 by their partner, but better known as a picnic spot and fisherman's access.

Nature Note ▪ Altitude Affects Vegetation: The Teton summits, supporting only the hardiest lichens, are too high for trees. This is due not to thin air but to climatic conditions. It's too cold, too windy, or the soil is too thin. Latitude also has an effect. For example, in the Canadian Rockies, timberline occurs around 6,500 feet above sea level, while in the more southerly climate of New Mexico, timberline is close to 12,000 feet. Here, trees rarely grow above 9,000 to 10,000 feet. ▪

Snake River Overlook: Perched above a wide bend in the river, this is perhaps the best-known view of the Tetons, particularly good early in the morning when mist is rising from the river. Look for osprey and bald eagles. From here you can see up Cascade Canyon to The Wigwams, a pyramidal peak above the forks of Cascade Creek. Lake Solitude is a long hike up the canyon on one of the park's more popular trails.

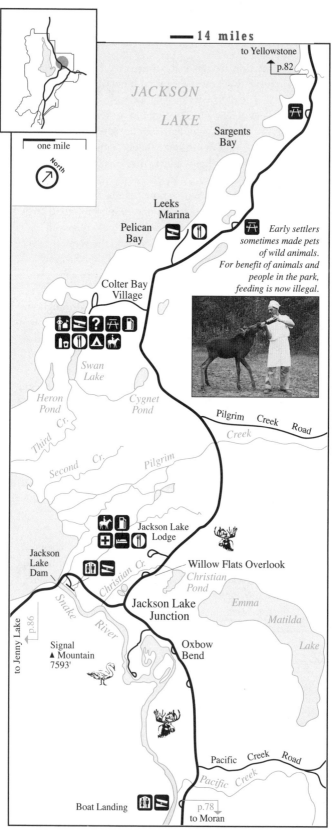

to Yellowstone
↑ p.82

JACKSON

LAKE

Sargents
Bay

one mile

North

Leeks
Marina

Pelican
Bay

*Early settlers
sometimes made pets
of wild animals.
For benefit of animals and
people in the park,
feeding is now illegal.*

Colter Bay
Village

*Swan
Lake*

*Heron
Pond*

*Cygnet
Pond*

Pilgrim   Creek   Road

Creek

Third   Cr.

Second   Cr.

Pilgrim

Jackson Lake
Lodge

Jackson
Lake
Dam

Christian Cr.

Willow Flats Overlook

*Christian
Pond*

Emma

Matilda

Jackson Lake
Junction

Lake

to Jenny Lake
← p.86

Snake   River

Signal
▲ Mountain
7593'

Oxbow
Bend

Pacific   Creek   Road

Pacific   Creek

Boat Landing

p.78 ↓
to Moran

80

Moran to Yellowstone

Leeks Marina: Stephen Leek settled beside Jackson Lake before the 1900s. His photographs of starving elk, cut off from traditional winter range, were instrumental in establishment of the National Elk Refuge.

Colter Bay: Full services are available here. The Indian Arts Museum, in the visitor center, has a noteworthy collection of artifacts, well presented (open mid-May to September). Short, easy trails in this area lead along the lakeshore, affording numerous mountain views.

Pilgrim Creek: Hurrying along a wide, boulder-strewn bottom, this creek drains the Teton Wilderness. A gravel road north of the creek ends after 3 miles, at the boundary between the national forest and the park. Beside the creek, spruce and fir trees thrive in moist soil. Farther from the water, the forest is lodgepole pine. Lodgepole, adapted to fire, is one of the first trees to grow after a burn. Then spruce and fir gradually take over. In much of this region, however, because soils are too dry or too poor to support spruce and fir, lodgepole is the so-called "climax" species.

Willow Flats Overlook: In autumn, the willows turn red-gold, carpeting the valley with color. There is a fine view of Jackson Lake with the central Tetons and Mount Moran. Skillet Glacier, appearing to have a long handle, is prominent on the face of Moran.

Oxbow Bend of the Snake: The Snake River makes a wide bend here, creating a series of ponds—cut-off river meanders. Although the river is still connected to these ponds, the main current takes a more direct route. Moose, otters, swans, osprey, bald eagles, herons, pelicans, geese, and ducks live here. When calm, the water reflects a classic view of the Teton Range. A dirt road just west of the turnout leads 1 mile to Cattleman's Bridge and an unmaintained trail that leads to the summit of Signal Mountain, looming just to the south.

Pacific Creek: A gravel road leads to the Pacific Creek Trailhead on the Teton Wilderness boundary (6 miles); it also leads to Two Ocean Lake (4 miles, no boat motors allowed), and other trailheads.

Boat Landing: From here, Deadmans Bar is an easy half-day float; to the landing at Moose takes a full day.

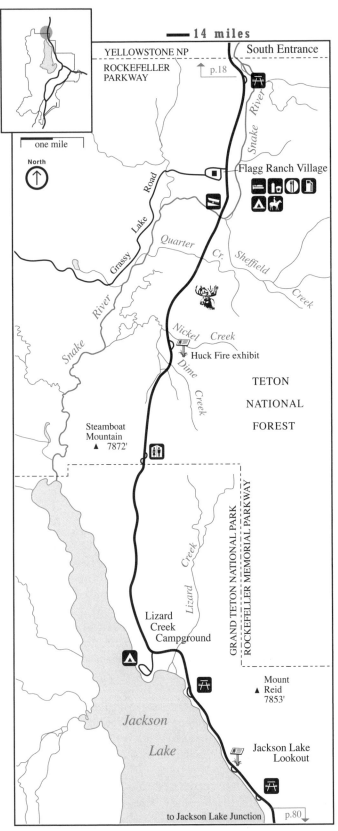

ROCKEFELLER
PARKWAY

p.18

one mile

North
↑

Road

Flagg Ranch Village

Lake

Grassy

Quarter

Cr.

Sheffield

River

Snake

Creek

Nickel Creek

Huck Fire exhibit

Dime Creek

TETON

NATIONAL

FOREST

Steamboat
Mountain
▲ 7872'

GRAND TETON NATIONAL PARK
ROCKEFELLER MEMORIAL PARKWAY

Creek

Lizard

Lizard
Creek
Campground

Mount
▲ Reid
7853'

Jackson

Lake

Jackson Lake
Lookout

to Jackson Lake Junction   p.80

Yellowstone Park, South Entrance: The Snake River flows out of wilderness at this point, having begun its journey outside Yellowstone's southeast corner—very near the source of the Yellowstone River. The Yellowstone flows north, then east, eventually joining the Missouri River on its way to the Gulf of Mexico. The Snake goes south and west toward the Columbia and the Pacific.

Grassy Lake Road: This rough gravel road leads about 45 miles west to Ashton, Idaho, winding through forest and meadow, passing several lakes including the Grassy Lake Reservoir. Not recommended for RVs and trailers; closed in winter.

Flagg Ranch Village: Visitor services include camping, lodging, gas, groceries, and other supplies.

John D. Rockefeller Memorial Parkway: Honoring Rockefeller's contribution to the establishment of Grand Teton National Park, this strip of land is set aside as a scenic corridor.

Lizard Creek Campground: There are no lizards in the park, but there are salamanders, and to the pioneer eye, a lizard was probably worth as much as a salamander. To a biologist, however, the difference is important. Salamanders are amphibians, and live in water. Lizards are reptiles, breathe air, and live on land.

Jackson Lake Lookout: Here on the lakeshore, travelers get their first or last clear view of the Teton Range, depending on the direction they are heading. Here the fault-block nature of the Tetons is evident. The mountains, on one block of the earth's crust, tilted up to create a steep rampart facing east, and a more gradual slope to the west. The neighboring block—now the valley called Jackson Hole, and including Jackson Lake—subsided. Total movement along the fault is estimated at 30,000 feet. Over time, the twin forces of erosion and glacial action have stripped off the higher layers, leaving a still-impressive 7,000-vertical-foot mountain escarpment.

Jackson Lake is a natural body of water enlarged to 26,000 acres by the Jackson Lake Dam, which raised the water level 39 feet. The original shoreline is several miles south of this overlook. An exhibit here tells about the 1974 Waterfalls Canyon Fire. The result is visible across the lake to the south.

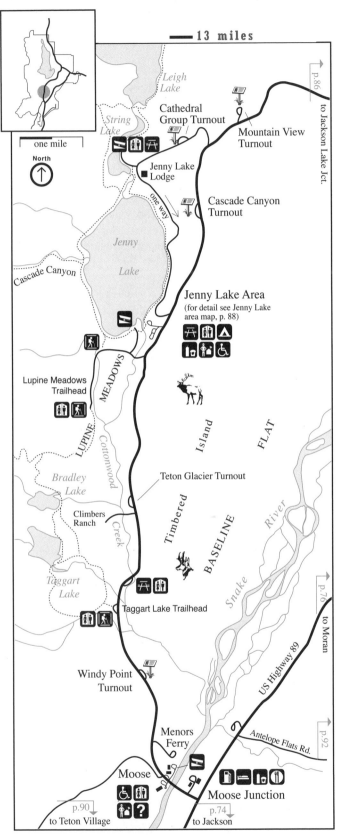

13 miles

Leigh Lake

String Lake

Cathedral Group Turnout

Mountain View Turnout

Jenny Lake Lodge

Jenny Lake

one way

Cascade Canyon Turnout

Cascade Canyon

Jenny Lake Area
(for detail see Jenny Lake area map, p. 88)

Lupine Meadows Trailhead

MEADOWS

LUPINE

Bradley Lake

Cottonwood Creek

Teton Glacier Turnout

Climbers Ranch

Island

FLAT

Timbered

BASELINE

Snake River

Taggart Lake

Taggart Lake Trailhead

Windy Point Turnout

US Highway 89

Menors Ferry

Antelope Flats Rd.

Moose

Moose Junction

to Teton Village

to Jackson

p.86
to Jackson Lake Jct.
p.76
to Moran
p.92
p.90
p.74

one mile

North

Teton Park Road

Lupine Meadows: A side road crosses Cottonwood Creek, providing access to the Jenny Lake boat launch, and two trailheads. One trail follows the lakeshore to Cascade Canyon and Hidden Falls. The second climbs to Garnet Canyon, the most popular approach for climbers attempting the Grand Teton, and to Amphitheater Lake about 3,000 feet above the valley floor.

Teton Glacier Turnout: The 13,770-foot Grand Teton is Wyoming's second highest peak. By official reckoning, the Grand was first climbed in 1898 by W. O. Owen, although others claimed to have done it earlier. What seems like the path of an enormous bulldozer on the lower half of the Grand is a gulch carved by a glacier during the last ice age. Today, the relatively small Teton Glacier shelters in the shade of the mountain's north face. Left of the Grand is the Middle Teton (12,804 feet), but what looks like it should be the South Teton is actually Nez Perce Peak (11,901 feet), hiding the South (12,514 feet) from view. To the right in the background is Mount Owen (12,928 feet), then craggy Teewinot (12,325 feet).

Taggart Lake Trailhead: A 1,028-acre forest fire burned the area to the west in 1985, providing an interesting comparison to areas that burned in Yellowstone in 1988, and revealing the shape of the morainal hills. Deposited by glaciers in Avalanche and Garnet Canyons, the moraines serve as dams to hold Bradley and Taggart Lakes. In winter, the road is closed beyond this point. From here, it is easy to understand why the trail to Jenny Lake is popular among cross-country skiers.

Windy Point Turnout: The Gros Ventre Slide is a prominent, reddish scar on Sleeping Indian Mountain across the valley. The slide occurred in 1925, creating a lake and causing a memorable flood two years later.

Menor's Ferry: William D. Menor homesteaded here in 1894 and built a cable ferry across the Snake River. His buildings and the ferry have been restored. Also here is the attractive, log Chapel of the Transfiguration.

Snake River: Scenic float trips through the park end just above the bridge, but the river is navigable almost to Palisades Reservoir, at the bottom of white-water-filled Snake River Canyon (south of Jackson Hole).

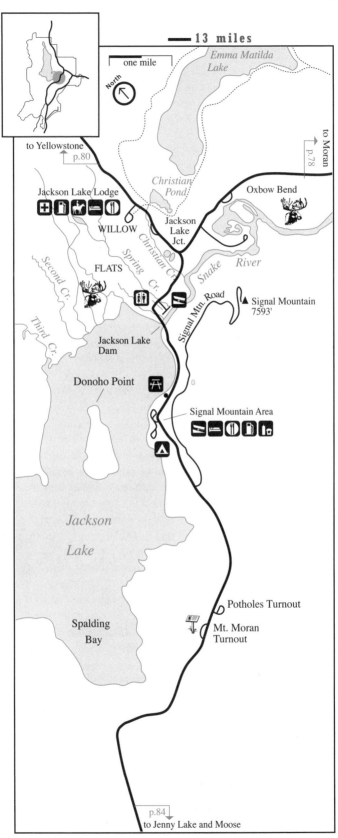

one mile

North

Emma Matilda Lake

to Yellowstone
p.80

to Moran
p.78

Christian Pond

Jackson Lake Lodge

Oxbow Bend

WILLOW

Jackson Lake Jct.

Spring Cr.

Christian Cr.

Snake   River

Second Cr.

FLATS

▲ Signal Mountain
7593'

Signal Mtn. Road

Third Cr.

Jackson Lake Dam

Donoho Point

Signal Mountain Area

Jackson

Lake

Spalding Bay

Potholes Turnout

Mt. Moran Turnout

p.84
to Jenny Lake and Moose

Jackson Lake Dam: Before human engineers got to work (in 1906), beavers were active here at the lake's outlet, creating numerous ponds that eventually filled in to become a wetland covered with shrubby willow. This is an excellent place to see moose, especially from the Willow Flats Overlook 4 miles north on the road to Yellowstone. The dam—the fourth one on this site—was rebuilt in 1989 to the same height as the previous one. It is interesting to keep in mind that over thousands of years, as glaciers have come and gone, and as the region's climate has shifted from moist to dry and back again, the lake has also risen and fallen, changing shape and draining from various points along its shoreline. No landscape is permanent. Looking far enough back in geologic history, there was a time when neither the lake nor the mountains existed.

Boat launch and fishing access are located immediately downstream of the dam, on the north bank.

Signal Mountain Road: This 5-mile paved road leads to the summit of Signal Mountain, some 1,000 feet above Jackson Lake. Because it stands away from the main range, Signal Mountain provides a grandstand view not only of the Tetons but of surrounding ranges as well. This is a good place to appreciate the geology of Jackson Hole—the steep mountains rising abruptly without foothills, the valley tilting slightly to the west, the Snake River winding through banks of rubble left behind by glaciers. The view is particularly fine at sunset. Trailers and RVs are not permitted because the road is narrow and turns are tight.

Mount Moran Turnout: The mountain, 12,605 feet high, was named for Thomas Moran, the landscape artist who accompanied General Washburn on the famous 1870 Yellowstone Expedition. Moran's paintings helped convince Congress to create the world's first national park.

From here, Hanging Ice Glacier is prominent on the mountain's east face. The summit (not as flat as it appears—it drops off steeply on the back side) retains a layer of the sandstone that once covered all the Teton Range before erosion stripped off the upper layers and carved the underlying granitic stone into its various peaks. There is a corresponding layer of sandstone some 24,000 feet below the valley surface—carried down on the subsiding block while the mountains rose.

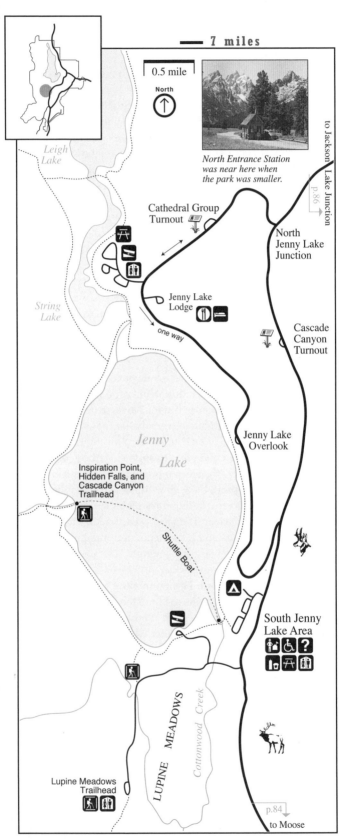

7 miles

0.5 mile

North ↑

North Entrance Station was near here when the park was smaller.

to Jackson Lake Junction

p.86

Leigh Lake

String Lake

Cathedral Group Turnout

North Jenny Lake Junction

Jenny Lake Lodge

one way

Cascade Canyon Turnout

Jenny Lake

Jenny Lake Overlook

Inspiration Point, Hidden Falls, and Cascade Canyon Trailhead

Shuttle Boat

South Jenny Lake Area

LUPINE MEADOWS

Cottonwood Creek

Lupine Meadows Trailhead

p.84

to Moose

Jenny Lake Area

Jenny Lake Road: The road climbs onto an old river terrace and winds through meadows to the scenic heart of the Tetons. This very popular area is best—and less crowded—early in the morning. Beyond the String Lake junction this becomes a one-way road.

Cathedral Group Turnout: From this vantage, Mount Owen, Teewinot and The Grand look like a single mountain—a cathedral with many spires, the north side plunging dramatically into Cascade Canyon. Counting northward from the canyon are the following peaks: Symmetry Spire, then Mount St. John (11,430 feet), Rockchuck Peak (11,144 feet), Mount Woodring (11,590 feet) in the background, Leigh Canyon, and then the great mass of Mount Moran (12,605 feet), with Falling Ice Glacier and the prominent volcanic Black Dike.

String Lake: Narrow, calm, and shallow, String Lake is a popular boating site (no motors). An easy trail leads north 1 mile to the shores of Leigh Lake, where the water is sometimes warm enough for swimming and the views of Mount Moran are unsurpassed. Canoeists can reach Leigh Lake by a short portage.

Jenny Lake Overlook: The road follows the terminal moraine created by a glacier that flowed out of Cascade Canyon. The moraine now serves as a dam of broken rock to contain Jenny Lake. Neighboring lakes—Leigh, String, Bradley, and others—were also created by glaciers, and are located at the mouths of canyons.

Jenny Lake: The second largest lake in Jackson Hole was named for Jenny Leigh, the Shoshone wife of trapper "Beaver Dick" Leigh. To many visitors, this is the heart of the Tetons. Passenger boats shuttle between the parking area and the Cascade Canyon Trailhead, where a trail climbs a half mile to lovely Hidden Falls, and on to Inspiration Point. Seven miles up the trail, on the other side of the Tetons, is Lake Solitude. One popular idea is to take the boat across, visit the falls, and then walk back along the lakeshore.

South Jenny Lake Area: From the parking area, trails go to the lake shore; facilities include a visitor center, ranger station, general store, boat rental, and boat rides across the lake to Cascade Canyon.

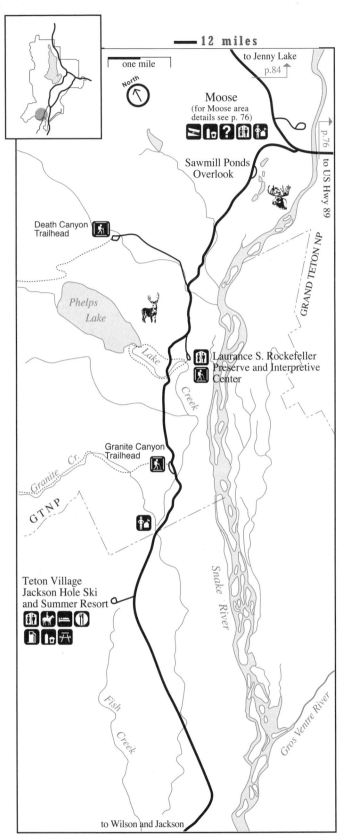

12 miles

one mile

North

to Jenny Lake
p.84

p.76

to US Hwy 89

Moose
(for Moose area
details see p. 76)

Sawmill Ponds
Overlook

Death Canyon
Trailhead

GRAND TETON NP

Phelps
Lake

Lake

Creek

Laurance S. Rockefeller
Preserve and Interpretive
Center

Granite Canyon
Trailhead

Granite Cr.

GTNP

Snake
River

Teton Village
Jackson Hole Ski
and Summer Resort

Fish

Creek

Gros Ventre River

to Wilson and Jackson

Moose to Teton Village

Moose Visitor Center: The visitor center is open year round, providing information, permits, and publications. Exhibits feature geology, history, and wildlife.

Moose–Wilson Road: This narrow, sometimes rough road rolls 8 miles through meadow and forest between Teton Village (Jackson Hole Ski Resort) and Moose Junction—this is not a short-cut to Wilson. Along the way, the Tetons pop in and out of view. Cold mountain streams tumble through ravines. Deer and elk graze in the meadows. Across the valley, the Gros Ventre Range is occasionally visible. There are many aspens, making for nice fall colors. The road also provides access to trailheads. *(Vehicles over 20 feet or one ton are prohibited. Closed in winter.)*

Sawmill Ponds Overlook: Among sagebrush and wildflowers, the overlook is perched on the edge of an old Snake River terrace. The spring-fed ponds and wetlands below are rich in wildlife—small and large. It's a relaxing place to spend a quiet hour with binoculars.

Death Canyon Trailhead: A paved road, turning to dirt, leads to the Whitegrass Ranger Station and the Death Canyon Trailhead. An easy mile up the trail is the Phelps Lake Overlook, a fine picnic spot. Beyond, the trail follows a more strenuous path into the upper meadows of Death Canyon and beyond. The canyon is a much more pleasant place than suggested by its name, which seems to have originated with the disappearance here of a member of an 1899 survey party.

JY Ranch: Now called the Laurance S. Rockefeller Preserve, this was one of the valley's first dude ranches. The Rockefeller family owned it for decades and donated it over to the public in 2001.

Granite Canyon: Starting at this parking area trails range from easy through rolling sage-covered hills to the strenuous ascent of Granite Canyon. Wildflowers are good in summer. On autumn evenings, bull elk can be heard bugling among the golden aspens.

Teton Village Resort: The tram carries hikers and sightseers or skiers depending on the season. A popular hike begins at the summit, circles around behind the mountain, and descends Granite Canyon.

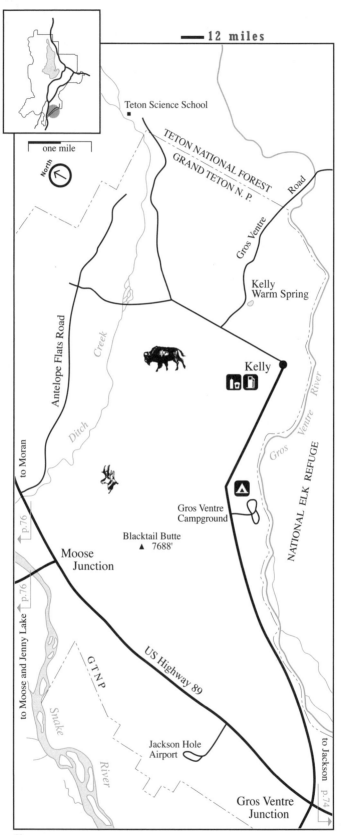

12 miles

Teton Science School

TETON NATIONAL FOREST

GRAND TETON N. P.

Gros Ventre Road

Kelly Warm Spring

Antelope Flats Road

Creek

Ditch

to Moran

p.76

Kelly

Gros Ventre River

NATIONAL ELK REFUGE

Gros Ventre Campground

Blacktail Butte
▲ 7688'

Moose Junction

to Moose and Jenny Lake

p.76

Snake

GTNP

US Highway 89

River

Jackson Hole Airport

to Jackson

p.74

Gros Ventre Junction

one mile

North

Kelly Road

Kelly Warm Spring: This lukewarm pond is a nice picnic spot, warm enough for swimming but with a muddy bottom. Tropical fish, released from aquariums, survive here year-round—a surprising sight in the decidedly untropical mountain west.

The Kelly Flood: May 18, 1927, is an important date in the history of the entire valley, but especially for the town of Kelly, Wyoming, which was wiped out by a flood that day. The story began two years earlier, in June 1925, when a cowboy named Huff, herding cattle along the Gros Ventre River, realized the mountain, trees and all, was sliding down toward him. He lost a few cattle but saved himself.

The slide, which left a mile-long scar visible from throughout the valley (but not from Kelly townsite), built a 225-foot dam, holding back the waters of a steadily growing lake. It took two years for the Gros Ventre to breach the dam. When it did, a wall of water swept down the canyon, destroying Kelly. Even the town of Wilson, across the valley at the base of Teton Pass, was submerged in 6 feet of water. Most valley residents managed to escape, but six were killed.

Nature Note ■ Tree Habitat: Notice the distribution of trees in Jackson Hole. Most of the valley is filled with glacial outwash—boulders and gravel through which water drains easily. Sagebrush, with its taproots probing deep below the surface, thrives on the valley floor, but trees do not. Trees occur only where moisture and soil conditions are adequate. Cottonwoods prefer river bottoms. Spruce and fir trees live on cool, north-facing slopes. Aspens grow on southern exposures but only if the soil retains enough moisture, which is rare in this part of the valley. ■

Gros Ventre River: Indians and trappers traveling between the Wind River Range and the Yellowstone area followed the valley of the Gros Ventre. When highways were built to Jackson Hole, engineers chose the current Hoback River route, which follows the next drainage to the south. Only a rough forest road follows the upper Gros Ventre today.

Index

Absaroka Mountains 57, 63
Antelope Creek 55
Apollinaris Spring 45
Arnica Creek 43

Barronette Peak 63
Beaver Lake 45
Biscuit Basin 25
Black Butte 69
Blacktail Butte 77
Blacktail Deer Creek 51
Blacktail Drive 51
Blacktail Ponds 77
Bridge Bay 9, 12, 41
Buffalo Fork River 79

Calcite Springs 53, 55
Canyon Village 10, 37, 57
Carrington Island 43
Cascade Creek 33, 35
Cathedral Group 89
Continental Divide 14, 21, 23, 51
Craig Pass 23
Cunningham Cabin 79

Deadmans Bar 79, 81
Death Canyon 77, 91
Divide Lake 69
Duck Lake 23
Dunraven Pass 57

East Entrance 67
Elk Antler Creek 39

Fire Exhibit 19, 33, 45, 47, 53, 59
Firehole Canyon Drive 29
Firehole River 25, 51, 29
Fishing Bridge 8, 12, 65
Flagg Ranch 9-11, 83
Flat Creek 75
Floating Island Lake 53
Fort Yellowstone 47
Fountain Paint Pot 29
Frying Pan Spring 45

Gallatin Ranger Station 69
Gallatin River 69
Gardner River 51
Gibbon Falls 31
Gibbon Geyser Basin 31
Glacier Gulch 85
Glacier View 77
Golden Gate 47
Granite Creek 91
Grant Village 8, 9, 21
Grayling Creek 69
Gros Ventre River 75, 93
Gros Ventre Slide 85

Hayden Valley 37, 39
Hedrick Pond 79
Hellroaring Mountain 53

Icebox Canyon 63

Indian Pond 65
Isa Lake 23

Jackson Lake 9-11, 81, 83, 87
Jenny Lake 10, 12, 85, 89
Jenny Lake Loop Road 89
JY Ranch 91

Kelly Warm Springs 93

Lake Butte 65
Lake Village 41
Lamar Glacier Turnout 61
Leeks Marina 81
Le Hardy Rapid 39
Lewis Lake 21
Lewis River 19
Lizard Creek 83
Lupine Meadows 85

Madison Canyon 59
Mammoth Hot Springs 10, 49, 51
Mary Bay 65
Menor's Ferry 85
Midway Geyser Basin 25
Moose Falls 19
Moose–Wilson Road 91
Moran Junction 79
Mount Everts 47, 51
Mount Haynes 59
Mount Hornaday 63
Mount Moran 71, 87, 89
Mount Sheridan 41, 43
Mud Volcano 39

National Elk Refuge 75, 81
National Fish Hatchery 75
Natural Bridge 41
Nez Perce Creek 29
Norris Geyser Basin 31, 45
Nymph Lake 45

Obsidian Cliff 45
Old Chittenden Road 55
Old Faithful 8, 9, 13, 16, 25, 51
Otter Creek 37
Oxbow Bend 81

Pacific Creek 81
Pebble Creek 63
Pelican Creek 65
Petrified Tree 53
Phantom Lake 51
Pilgrim Creek 81
Pleasant Valley 61
Potts Hot Springs 43
Pumice Point 43

Roaring Mountain 45
Rockefeller Memorial Pkwy. 83
Roosevelt Lodge 10, 53
Round Prairie 63

Sawmill Ponds 91
Scaup Lake 23
Sedge Creek 65

Sheepeater Cliff 47
Shoshone Point 23
Signal Mountain 9, 11, 81, 87
Snake River 9, 70, 71, 75, 77, 79, 81, 83, 85, 87, 91, 21
Snake River Overlook 79
Soda Butte 63
South Entrance 83, 19
Specimen Creek 69
Spread Creek 79
Steamboat Point 21, 65
String Lake 89
Sulphur Caldron 39
Sylvan Pass 67

Taggart Lake 85
Terrace Spring 31
Teton Point 77
Teton Village 91
The Thunderer 63
Tower Creek 55, 57
Tower Soldier Station 53
Trout Creek 39

Twin Lakes 45

Undine Falls 51
Upper Falls 35, 51
Upper Geyser Basin 25, 27

Virginia Cascade 33

Warm Creek 51
Washburn Range 33, 37, 57
West Entrance 59
West Thumb Geyser Basin 21, 43, 65
Willow Flats 81, 87
Willow Park 45
Windy Point 85
Wolves 61
Wraith Falls 51

Yancey Creek 53
Yellowstone Lake 9, 21, 23, 41, 43
Yellowstone River 9, 83, 17, 33, 35, 37, 39, 55, 61

Further Reading
For Yellowstone

Bartlett, Richard A. Yellowstone, *A Wilderness Besieged*. University of Arizona Press, Tucson, AZ, 1989.

Haines, Aubrey L. *The Yellowstone Story*. University Press of Colorado, Boulder, CO, 1996.

Marschall, Mark C. *Yellowstone Trails: A Hiking Guide*. Yellowstone Association, 1999.

Russell, Osborne. *Journal of a Trapper*. Aubrey L. Haines, Ed. University of Nebraska Press, Lincoln, NE, 1965.

Schullery, Paul. *Mountain Time: A Yellowstone Memoir*. Robert Rinehart Publishers, Boulder, CO, 2000.

_____. *The Bears of Yellowstone* (revised edition), Roberts Rinehart Publishers, Boulder, CO, 1992.

_____. *Searching for Yellowstone: Ecology and Wonder in the Last Wilderness*. Houghton Mifflin Co., Boston, MA, 1997.

Whittlesey, Lee H. *Yellowstone Place Names*. Montana Historical Society Press, 1988.

For Grand Teton

Bywater and Olson. *A Guide to Exploring Grand Teton NP*. RNM Press, Salt Lake City, UT, 1995.

McNulty, Tim. *Grand Teton National Park: Where Lightning Walks*. Woodlands Press, Del Mar, CA, 1986.

McPhee, John. *Rising From the Plains*. Farrar, Straus & Giroux, New York, 1987.

Murie, Margaret and Olaus. *Wapiti Wilderness: The Life of Olaus and Margaret Murie in Jackson Hole, Wyoming*. University Press of Colorado, Boulder, CO, 1987.

Raynes, Bert. *Birds of Grand Teton National Park and Surrounding Area*. Grand Teton NHA, Moose, WY, 1986.

Steven Fuller has been the Winterkeeper and a year-round resident at the Grand Canyon of the Yellowstone River in the heart of Yellowstone Park since 1973. His Yellowstone photographs and writings have appeared in many books and magazines, including National Geographic, and have received awards both in the United States and England.

Jeremy Schmidt spent seven years living in Yellowstone, working as a winterkeeper, ranger and photographer. Now living in Jackson Hole, Wyoming, he writes for magazines including *National Geographic, GEO, International Wildlife,* and others. His book *Himalayan Passage: Seven Months in the High Country of Tibet, Nepal, China, India, and Pakistan* (The Mountaineers Books) was the winner of the 1991 Barbara Savage Award for adventure writing.

Jeremy Schmidt, *2010 update*
Wendy Baylor and Jeremy Schmidt,
    Computer composition and design for original edition
Wendy Baylor, *Maps*
Jocelyn Slack, *Illustrations*
Yellowstone and Grand Teton National Parks, *Photos*

National Geographic Travel Books
Caroline Hickey, *Project Manager*
Cinda Rose, *Art Director*
Bea Jackson, *Cover Design*
Greg Ugiansky, *Map Production*

ISBN: 978-1-4262-0597-2

The Library of Congress cataloged the 2004 edition as follows:

Schmidt, Jeremy, 1949-
National Geographic Yellowstone Grand Teton road guide : the essential guide for motorists / by Jeremy Schmidt and Steven Fuller.
    p. cm.
Includes bibliographical references (p.) and index.
  ISBN 0-7922-6639-0
  1. Yellowstone National Park--Guidebooks. 2. Grand Teton National Park (Wyo.)--Guidebooks. 3. Automobile travel--Yellowstone National Park--Guidebooks. 4. Automobile travel--Wyoming--Grand Teton National Park--Guidebooks. I. Title: Yellowstone Grand Teton road guide. II. Fuller, Steven. III. National Geographic Society (U.S.) IV. Title.
  F722.S35 2003   2003022222
  917.87'5204--dc22

Printed in U.S.A.   10/WOR/2